CESARE BORGIA

CESARE BORGIA

John Haney

1987
CHELSEA HOUSE PUBLISHERS
NEW YORK
NEW HAVEN   PHILADELPHIA

23270

EDITORIAL DIRECTOR: Nancy Toff
MANAGING EDITOR: Karyn Gullen Browne
COPY CHIEF: Perry Scott King
ART DIRECTOR: Giannella Garrett
ASSISTANT ART DIRECTOR: Carol McDougall
PICTURE EDITOR: Elizabeth Terhune

Staff for CESARE BORGIA:

SENIOR EDITOR: John W. Selfridge
ASSISTANT EDITORS: Maria Behan, Pierre Hauser, Howard Ratner, Bert Yaeger
COPY EDITORS: Sean Dolan, Kathleen McDermott
ASSISTANT DESIGNER: Noreen Lamb
PICTURE RESEARCH: Susan Quist
LAYOUT: David Murray
PRODUCTION COORDINATOR: Alma Rodriguez
PRODUCTION ASSISTANT: Karen Dreste
COVER ILLUSTRATION: Richard Leonard

CREATIVE DIRECTOR: Harold Steinberg

Frontispiece courtesy of The Bettmann Archive

First Printing

Library of Congress Cataloging in Publication Data

Haney, John D. CESARE BORGIA

(World leaders past & present)
Bibliography: p.
Includes index.
1. Borgia, Cesare, 1476?–1507—Juvenile literature.
2. Papal States—History—Julius II, 1503–1513—Juvenile
literature. 3. Italy—History—1492–1559—Juvenile literature.
4. Papal States—Nobility—Biography—Juvenile literature.
[1. Borgia, Cesare, 1476?–1507. 2. Italy—History—
1492–1559]
I. Title. II. Series.
DG797.82.H36   1985   945'.606'0924 [92]   85-19034

ISBN 0-87754-595-2

Contents

ADENAUER
ALEXANDER THE GREAT
MARC ANTONY
KING ARTHUR
ATATÜRK
ATTLEE
BEGIN
BEN-GURION
BISMARCK
LÉON BLUM
BOLÍVAR
CESARE BORGIA
BRANDT
BREZHNEV
CAESAR
CALVIN
CASTRO
CATHERINE THE GREAT
CHARLEMAGNE
CHIANG KAI-SHEK
CHURCHILL
CLEMENCEAU
CLEOPATRA
CORTÉS
CROMWELL
DANTON
DE GAULLE
DE VALERA
DISRAELI
EISENHOWER
ELEANOR OF AQUITAINE
QUEEN ELIZABETH I
FERDINAND AND ISABELLA
FRANCO

FREDERICK THE GREAT
INDIRA GANDHI
MOHANDAS GANDHI
GARIBALDI
GENGHIS KHAN
GLADSTONE
GORBACHEV
HAMMARSKJÖLD
HENRY VIII
HENRY OF NAVARRE
HINDENBURG
HITLER
HO CHI MINH
HUSSEIN
IVAN THE TERRIBLE
ANDREW JACKSON
JEFFERSON
JOAN OF ARC
POPE JOHN XXIII
LYNDON JOHNSON
JUÁREZ
JOHN F. KENNEDY
KENYATTA
KHOMEINI
KHRUSHCHEV
MARTIN LUTHER KING, JR.
KISSINGER
LENIN
LINCOLN
LLOYD GEORGE
LOUIS XIV
LUTHER
JUDAS MACCABEUS
MAO ZEDONG

MARY, QUEEN OF SCOTS
GOLDA MEIR
METTERNICH
MUSSOLINI
NAPOLEON
NASSER
NEHRU
NERO
NICHOLAS II
NIXON
NKRUMAH
PERICLES
PERÓN
QADDAFI
ROBESPIERRE
ELEANOR ROOSEVELT
FRANKLIN D. ROOSEVELT
THEODORE ROOSEVELT
SADAT
STALIN
SUN YAT-SEN
TAMERLANE
THATCHER
TITO
TROTSKY
TRUDEAU
TRUMAN
VICTORIA
WASHINGTON
WEIZMANN
WOODROW WILSON
XERXES
ZHOU ENLAI

ON LEADERSHIP
Arthur M. Schlesinger, jr.

LEADERSHIP, it may be said, is really what makes the world go round. Love no doubt smooths the passage; but love is a private transaction between consenting adults. Leadership is a public transaction with history. The idea of leadership affirms the capacity of individuals to move, inspire, and mobilize masses of people so that they act together in pursuit of an end. Sometimes leadership serves good purposes, sometimes bad; but whether the end is benign or evil, great leaders are those men and women who leave their personal stamp on history.

Now, the very concept of leadership implies the proposition that individuals can make a difference. This proposition has never been universally accepted. From classical times to the present day, eminent thinkers have regarded individuals as no more than the agents and pawns of larger forces, whether the gods and goddesses of the ancient world or, in the modern era, race, class, nation, the dialectic, the will of the people, the spirit of the times, history itself. Against such forces, the individual dwindles into insignificance.

So contends the thesis of historical determinism. Tolstoy's great novel *War and Peace* offers a famous statement of the case. Why, Tolstoy asked, did millions of men in the Napoleonic wars, denying their human feelings and their common sense, move back and forth across Europe slaughtering their fellows? "The war," Tolstoy answered, "was bound to happen simply because it was bound to happen." All prior history predetermined it. As for leaders, they, Tolstoy said, "are but the labels that serve to give a name to an end and, like labels, they have the least possible connection with the event." The greater the leader, "the more conspicuous the inevitability and the predestination of every act he commits." The leader, said Tolstoy, is "the slave of history."

Determinism takes many forms. Marxism is the determinism of class. Nazism the determinism of race. But the idea of men and women as the slaves of history runs athwart the deepest human instincts. Rigid determinism abolishes the idea of human freedom—

the assumption of free choice that underlies every move we make, every word we speak, every thought we think. It abolishes the idea of human responsibility, since it is manifestly unfair to reward or punish people for actions that are by definition beyond their control. No one can live consistently by any deterministic creed. The Marxist states prove this themselves by their extreme susceptibility to the cult of leadership.

More than that, history refutes the idea that individuals make no difference. In December 1931 a British politician crossing Park Avenue in New York City between 76th and 77th Streets around 10:30 P.M. looked in the wrong direction and was knocked down by an automobile—a moment, he later recalled, of a man aghast, a world aglare: "I do not understand why I was not broken like an eggshell or squashed like a gooseberry." Fourteen months later an American politician, sitting in an open car in Miami, Florida, was fired on by an assassin; the man beside him was hit. Those who believe that individuals make no difference to history might well ponder whether the next two decades would have been the same had Mario Constasino's car killed Winston Churchill in 1931 and Giuseppe Zangara's bullet killed Franklin Roosevelt in 1933. Suppose, in addition, that Adolf Hitler had been killed in the street fighting during the Munich *Putsch* of 1923 and that Lenin had died of typhus during World War I. What would the 20th century be like now?

For better or for worse, individuals do make a difference. "The notion that a people can run itself and its affairs anonymously," wrote the philosopher William James, "is now well known to be the silliest of absurdities. Mankind does nothing save through initiatives on the part of inventors, great or small, and imitation by the rest of us—these are the sole factors in human progress. Individuals of genius show the way, and set the patterns, which common people then adopt and follow."

Leadership, James suggests, means leadership in thought as well as in action. In the long run, leaders in thought may well make the greater difference to the world. But, as Woodrow Wilson once said, "Those only are leaders of men, in the general eye, who lead in action. . . . It is at their hands that new thought gets its translation into the crude language of deeds." Leaders in thought often invent in solitude and obscurity, leaving to later generations the tasks of imitation. Leaders in action—the leaders portrayed in this series—have to be effective in their own time.

And they cannot be effective by themselves. They must act in response to the rhythms of their age. Their genius must be adapted, in a phrase of William James's, "to the receptivities of the moment." Leaders are useless without followers. "There goes the mob," said the French politician hearing a clamor in the streets. "I am their leader. I must follow them." Great leaders turn the inchoate emotions of the mob to purposes of their own. They seize on the opportunities of their time, the hopes, fears, frustrations, crises, potentialities. They succeed when events have prepared the way for them, when the community is awaiting to be aroused, when they can provide the clarifying and organizing ideas. Leadership ignites the circuit between the individual and the mass and thereby alters history.

It may alter history for better or for worse. Leaders have been responsible for the most extravagant follies and most monstrous crimes that have beset suffering humanity. They have also been vital in such gains as humanity has made in individual freedom, religious and racial tolerance, social justice and respect for human rights.

There is no sure way to tell in advance who is going to lead for good and who for evil. But a glance at the gallery of men and women in *World Leaders—Past and Present* suggests some useful tests.

One test is this: do leaders lead by force or by persuasion? By command or by consent? Through most of history leadership was exercised by the divine right of authority. The duty of followers was to defer and to obey. "Theirs not to reason why,/ Theirs but to do and die." On occasion, as with the so-called "enlightened despots" of the 18th century in Europe, absolutist leadership was animated by humane purposes. More often, absolutism nourished the passion for domination, land, gold and conquest and resulted in tyranny.

The great revolution of modern times has been the revolution of equality. The idea that all people should be equal in their legal condition has undermined the old structure of authority, hierarchy and deference. The revolution of equality has had two contrary effects on the nature of leadership. For equality, as Alexis de Tocqueville pointed out in his great study *Democracy in America*, might mean equality in servitude as well as equality in freedom.

"I know of only two methods of establishing equality in the political world," Tocqueville wrote. "Rights must be given to every citizen, or none at all to anyone . . . save one, who is the master of all." There was no middle ground "between the sovereignty of all and the absolute power of one man." In his astonishing prediction of 20th-century totalitarian dictatorship, Tocqueville explained how the revolution of equality could lead to the *"Führerprinzip"* and more terrible absolutism than the world had ever known.

But when rights are given to every citizen and the sovereignty of all is established, the problem of leadership takes a new form, becomes more exacting than ever before. It is easy to issue commands and enforce them by the rope and the stake, the concentration camp and the *gulag.* It is much harder to use argument and achievement to overcome opposition and win consent. The Founding Fathers of the United States understood the difficulty. They believed that history had given them the opportunity to decide, as Alexander Hamilton wrote in the first Federalist Paper, whether men are indeed capable of basing government on "reflection and choice, or whether they are forever destined to depend . . . on accident and force."

Government by reflection and choice called for a new style of leadership and a new quality of followership. It required leaders to be responsive to popular concerns, and it required followers to be active and informed participants in the process. Democracy does not eliminate emotion from politics; sometimes it fosters demagoguery; but it is confident that, as the greatest of democratic leaders put it, you cannot fool all of the people all of the time. It measures leadership by results and retires those who overreach or falter or fail.

It is true that in the long run despots are measured by results too. But they can postpone the day of judgment, sometimes indefinitely, and in the meantime they can do infinite harm. It is also true that democracy is no guarantee of virtue and intelligence in government, for the voice of the people is not necessarily the voice of God. But democracy, by assuring the right of opposition, offers built-in resistance to the evils inherent in absolutism. As the theologian Reinhold Niebuhr summed it up, "Man's capacity for justice makes democracy possible, but man's inclination to injustice makes democracy necessary."

A second test for leadership is the end for which power is sought. When leaders have as their goal the supremacy of a master race or the promotion of totalitarian revolution or the acquisition and exploitation of colonies or the protection of greed and privilege or the preservation of personal power, it is likely that their leadership will do little to advance the cause of humanity. When their goal is the abolition of slavery, the liberation of women, the enlargement of opportunity for the poor and powerless, the extension of equal rights to racial minorities, the defense of the freedoms of expression and opposition, it is likely that their leadership will increase the sum of human liberty and welfare.

Leaders have done great harm to the world. They have also conferred great benefits. You will find both sorts in this series. Even "good" leaders must be regarded with a certain wariness. Leaders are not demigods; they put on their trousers one leg after another just like ordinary mortals. No leader is infallible, and every leader needs to be reminded of this at regular intervals. Irreverence irritates leaders but is their salvation. Unquestioning submission corrupts leaders and demands followers. Making a cult of a leader is always a mistake. Fortunately hero worship generates its own antidote. "Every hero," said Emerson, "becomes a bore at last."

The signal benefit the great leaders confer is to embolden the rest of us to live according to our own best selves, to be active, insistent, and resolute in affirming our own sense of things. For great leaders attest to the reality of human freedom against the supposed inevitabilities of history. And they attest to the wisdom and power that may lie within the most unlikely of us, which is why Abraham Lincoln remains the supreme example of great leadership. A great leader, said Emerson, exhibits new possibilities to all humanity. "We feed on genius. . . . Great men exist that there may be greater men."

Great leaders, in short, justify themselves by emancipating and empowering their followers. So humanity struggles to master its destiny, remembering with Alexis de Tocqueville: "It is true that around every man a fatal circle is traced beyond which he cannot pass; but within the wide verge of that circle he is powerful and free; as it is with man, so with communities."

—*New York*

1

The Exercise of Virtue

Shortly after dawn on December 31, 1502, a company of horsemen reined in their steeds on the banks of the Metaurus River a few miles south of Fano, a small town on Italy's Adriatic coast. With a precision born of long practice they tested the weapons they might be called upon to use later that same day, running their razor-sharp swords back and forth in their scabbards, slashing at the roadside vegetation with effortless strokes.

The man who had engaged their services, Cesare Borgia, illegitimate son of the reigning pope, the Spaniard Alexander VI, sat astride a magnificent charger a few yards from his team of hired killers, talking with his favorites and his household staff.

Cesare realized that his band probably considered him one of the harshest commanders for whom they had ever agreed to fight. As far as he was concerned, however, they could think as they wished. They were there to do his bidding, to fear and respect him.

Cesare smiled as he recalled how his spies had punished any Roman citizens foolish enough to criticize him: cutting out tongues and chopping off hands. Many enemies of the Borgias who thought themselves protected by their political connections

> *A man can do anything if he wills.*
> —LEON BATTISTA ALBERTI
> 15th-century
> Italian humanist

A 16th-century portrait of Cesare Borgia conveys a powerful impression of the self-assurance and cold-blooded ruthlessness that characterized his life.

ITALY IN THE 15TH CENTURY

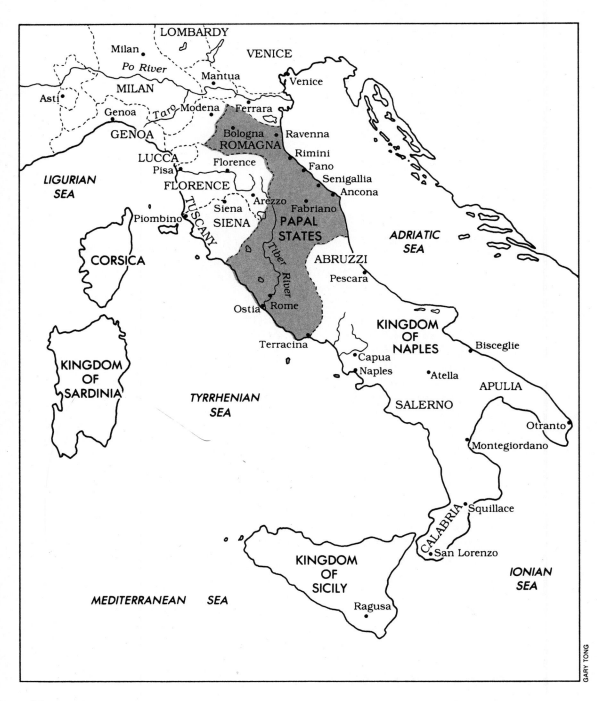

GARY TONG

THE PAPAL STATES

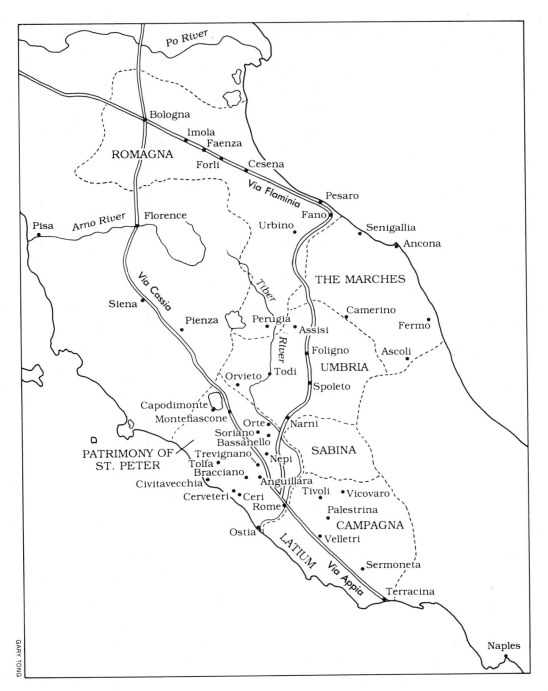

Po River

Bologna
Imola
Faenza
ROMAGNA
Forli   Cesena
Via Flaminia
Pesaro
Fano

Pisa   Arno River   Florence   Urbino
Senigallia
Ancona

Via Cassia
THE MARCHES

Siena   Camerino
Pienza   Perugia   Fermo
Tiber   Assisi
Foligno   Ascoli
Orvieto   Todi   UMBRIA
River   Spoleto

Capodimonte
Montefiascone   Orte   Narni
Soriano
Bassanello   SABINA
PATRIMONY OF   Trevignano   Nepi
ST. PETER   Tolfa
Bracciano
Civitavecchia   Anguillara
Cerveteri   Ceri   Tivoli   Vicovaro
Rome   Palestrina
Ostia   CAMPAGNA
Velletri
LATIUM   Via Appia   Sermoneta

Terracina

Naples

had been strangled and their corpses dumped in the Tiber River. As a contemporary historian wrote: "Men were safe neither in their rooms, nor their houses, nor their castles. The laws of God and man were as nothing. Gold, violence, and lust held undisputed sway."

Cesare Borgia made even his friends nervous. Mention of his name, or news that he was close by, could reduce his enemies to terror. During the previous 10 years he had played the game of Italian politics better than many of his competitors. On this day — December 31, 1502 — Cesare Borgia intended to surpass his previous atrocities before the new year was more than a few hours old.

German mercenaries such as those portrayed in this 16th-century engraving fought for Cesare during the campaigns he conducted to restore the Roman Catholic church's supremacy in the Papal States.

Out of the distance there came the sound of marching feet and the thudding of horses' hooves on frozen earth. Dressed in bright armor, Cesare turned to face his men-at-arms. His angular, handsome features were as if they had been carved from marble.

Pouring out from bridle paths and side roads came the rest of Cesare's army. Italian infantry, Swiss pikemen, German halberdiers, and several squadrons of cavalry moved into formation, and then stood stock-still as their officers rode to the head of the column to receive their orders. After a short briefing, Cesare dismissed them and gave the signal for the southward march to begin.

Cesare's destination was the castle on the Adriatic coast at Senigallia. Awaiting him there were several *condottieri* (mercenary captains) who had served him on a previous campaign. Following the campaign, the condottieri had tried to undermine Cesare's influence in the territories that he had conquered. They had plotted against him — and Cesare had pretended to forgive them. Having allowed them to continue in his service, he had directed them to take possession of Senigallia in preparation for his official entry. The tone in his communications to them had been like that of an indulgent parent scolding wayward children for minor misbehavior. Today, however, the game was up. The punishment, long overdue, would fit the crime.

The central Italian city-state of San Marino, where Cesare massed elements of his forces in preparation for his brilliant assault on the neighboring duchy of Urbino in June 1502.

17

As Cesare's soldiers closed in on Senigallia, the condottieri came out to greet him. Cesare, sensing that they feared him, tried to put them at ease by engaging them in cheerful conversation. The condottieri, however, remained terrified.

Informed by a messenger that Cesare needed every house in the town for quartering his own forces, the condottieri had dismissed their troops to positions several miles from Senigallia. Cesare's request had shocked the condottieri, for they had been led to believe that his forces were too inferior to threaten their own. Indeed, just 10 days earlier, their agents had told them that Cesare's French commanders had returned to Milan on the orders of their monarch, King Louis XII. It had been rumored, moreover, that the pope was growing tired of footing the bill for an army that was supposed to be fighting for the Church but which had seen no action in more than two months. The presence of Cesare and his army in Senigallia meant only one thing: the condottieri had been deceived.

Dismissing his entourage, Cesare led the condottieri to a house in the shadow of the castle walls. There he outlined his strategy for the next round of hostilities. Suddenly the curtains at one end of the chamber flew apart and armed men rushed in. Mailed fists and booted feet went to work on the helpless condottieri. Bruised and bloodied, Cesare's victims were dragged from the building and thrown into the dungeons.

Later that night — at 2:00 A.M. on January 1, 1503 — Cesare watched as two of the men who had insulted his intelligence by imagining they could betray him were put to death. Under the supervision of Miguel da Corella, Cesare's sadistic henchman, Oliverotto Eufreducci and Vitellozzo Vitelli were slowly strangled with silken cords.

When the deed was done, and while the other prisoners lay shivering in their cells, Cesare returned to his apartments. There he began the first of several letters to some of the most prominent men in Italy. He explained that the condottieri had betrayed him not once, but twice. They had expected him to come to Senigallia with just a few retainers. How-

The struggle by which Italy's tyrants established their tyranny, the efforts by which they defended it against foreign foes and domestic adversaries, trained them to endurance and daring. They lived habitually in an atmosphere of peril which taxed all their energies. Their activity was extreme, and their passions corresponded to their vehement vitality. About such men there could be nothing on a small or mediocre scale.
—JOHN ADDINGTON SYMONDS
19th-century
British historian

ever, with the aid of his intelligence services, he had discovered their true intentions, their plans to undermine and even usurp his authority.

Thus, Cesare wrote, he had gone to Senigallia not just to claim the city for the Church but also to have his revenge on the men who had planned to kill him. Their intended victim had arrived not with a handful of servants but at the head of an army. Two of his would-be murderers had died within hours of his entry into the town. Of the other three, Paolo and Francesco Orsini would meet their deaths at the hands of Cesare's henchmen within a few weeks, and Roberto Orsini would go free.

This Italian painting graphically illustrates the hideous conditions of many Renaissance prisons. On New Year's Day, 1503, Cesare Borgia visited one such prison to witness the torture and murder of two of his enemies.

ALINARI/ART RESOURCE

Following his first encounter with Cesare in June 1502, Florentine diplomat and political philosopher Niccolò Machiavelli came to consider him the model Italian ruler of his day.

Cesare knew that to men of his class and background such triumph over traitors would seem magnificent. Not his cruelty, but his genius for deception, would amaze them.

To 15th-century Italy's upper classes little mattered but power. According to their code of conduct, plotting a man's death was no crime. But failing to kill a man because of incompetence was unforgivable. Because Cesare was, in a way, one of the most perfect expressions of the age, he later emerged as the model Italian ruler of his day in a book written by Niccolò Machiavelli, the Florentine ambassador to his court.

In *The Prince* — which is still required reading for most students of politics today — Machiavelli advised rulers on how best to govern. He outlined a set of principles based on the conclusions that he had drawn from his personal observations of the political situation in Italy, analyzing the successes and failures of the great leaders of his day. One

Italian leader in particular fascinated Machiavelli from the moment that he met him—Cesare Borgia.

Much of the controversy that still surrounds Machiavelli's masterpiece centers upon the fact that it seems to justify the actions of men like Cesare. However, pronouncements that we might consider shocking today begin to make sense if we understand that they were appropriate to the time and place in which they were made. Machiavelli firmly believed that a prince should not worry about charges of cruelty, since "by making an example or two he will prove more compassionate than those who, being too compassionate, allow disorders which lead to murder and rapine. These nearly always harm the whole community, whereas executions ordered by a prince only affect individuals." When Machiavelli proposed that a prince "should not deviate from what is good, if that is possible, but he should know how to do evil if that is necessary," he was suggesting a way out of the kind of difficult situation that political leaders often encounter. In *The Prince*, Machiavelli presents Cesare Borgia as the embodiment of the two types of politician that preoccupy him throughout the book — the typical late 15th-century Italian ruler, achieving supremacy by rejecting all ethical considerations, and the reforming statesman.

It is interesting to note that Cesare ultimately achieved far less than might be imagined from Machiavelli's portrait. Ultimately, Cesare's importance as the model for Machiavelli's ideal prince vastly outweighs his actual historical importance.

The measures to which the Borgias resorted in their attempts to change the face of Italy were no different from those employed by their opponents. Given the times in which they lived, it is unreasonable to consider them monsters. However, neither their story nor *The Prince* makes for comforting reading. In the introduction to his translation of *The Prince*, British historian George Bull writes: "Most of the excitement and repulsion that *The Prince* has generated comes from its frank acknowledgement that in practice successful governments are always ready to act ruthlessly to attain their

> *It is not necessary that a prince should be merciful, loyal, humane, religious, just: nay, I will venture to say that if he had all these qualities and always used them, they would harm him. But he must seem to have them, especially if he be new in his principality, where he will find it quite impossible to exercise these virtues, since in order to maintain his power he will be often obliged to act contrary to humanity, charity, religion.*
> —NICCOLÒ MACHIAVELLI
> Florentine diplomat, historian, and political philosopher

ends." Like *The Prince*, the story of Cesare Borgia is capable of generating both excitement and disgust. That story begins 27 years before the events at Senigallia, in Rome.

In September 1475, in a small house on Rome's Via del Pellegrino, the 32-year-old wife of a lawyer gave birth to a son. Vannozza de' Cattanei and her elderly husband, Domenico da Rignano, were overjoyed at the infant's safe arrival. Medical practices were still primitive in those days, and childbirth was often a dangerous business.

Vannozza and da Rignano, however, had other reasons for feeling elated. This baby was more than just another mouth to feed. He represented their passport to comfort and security. For Vannozza, her second son was a priceless gift, her first child by a man she had adored for two years — not her husband, but a short, somewhat overweight, and rather ugly Spanish churchman named Rodrigo Borgia. Like many high-ranking clergymen at that time, Cardinal Borgia was neither celibate nor humble. He made vast amounts of money and had no objection in principle to the idea of making more. Rodrigo named his son Cesare, the Italian variant of Caesar, which was the family name of Julius Caesar, the Roman soldier and statesman who made himself dictator in 46 B.C. The name had become identified with absolutism since the dictator's death.

To da Rignano, his wife's relationship with this prominent churchman was welcome news. Association with the powerful was the surest route to social advancement in 15th-century Italy, and da Rignano's law practice had prospered during Rodrigo's affair with Vannozza. Rodrigo had known that securing da Rignano profitable employment within the Church administration would dispel whatever objections he may have had about the cardinal's relationship with his wife.

At the time of Cesare's birth, Rodrigo possessed numerous profitable benefices (paid ecclesiastical appointments) throughout Italy and his native Spain. Many of these archbishoprics and dioceses were held *in commendam*, which meant that he received the revenues accruing to the abbeys and churches of which he was titular head while rarely attending to their administration. He controlled castles that commanded some of the most important roads leading into Rome. He was also vice-chancellor of the Roman Catholic church — a very high position in a powerful organization.

At that time, the Roman Catholic church was in many ways similar to a modern business corporation. The Church owned substantial amounts of land throughout the Holy Roman Empire, a vast tract of western and central European territory covering much of present-day Austria, Belgium, Czechoslovakia, Germany, eastern France, the Netherlands, and northern Italy.

The first Holy Roman Empire had been established in 800, when Charlemagne, king of the Franks, was crowned emperor by Pope Leo III. Frederick I Barbarossa, who became emperor in 1155, believed that the empire had been established by God and that it was as important an institution as the Roman Catholic church. Frederick II, Barbarossa's successor, met with little success in his efforts to make the empire the greatest secular power in Europe, mainly because the popes regarded the empire as a threat to the influence of the Church.

By the time Cesare was born, the popes had been spending vast amounts of time, money, and energy in maintaining the Church's political and spiritual supremacy in the face of the threat represented by the Holy Roman Empire. Competition between the two powers had been going on for more than 500 years. During that period, the papacy had emerged, in the words of historian Roland H. Bainton, as "something between an Italian city-state and a European power, without forgetting at the same time the claim to be the vice-regent of Christ." "The pope," he wrote, "often could not make up his own mind whether he was the successor of [St.] Peter or Caesar."

The Church imposed an annual tax, known as "Peter's pence," on every household in Christendom. In addition to this tax, every Catholic had to pay a *tithe*, a tax amounting to 10 percent of his or

Born during the resurgence of interest in the cultures of ancient Greece and Rome that characterized the Renaissance, Cesare Borgia was named after Rome's first dictator, Julius Caesar. As Cesare grew into an unscrupulous and ambitious young man, his parents' choice of namesake seemed increasingly appropriate.

her income, which was used to support the local parish church. The revenues from these sources had made the Catholic church extremely rich. With power and prosperity, however, came avarice, immorality, and spiritual decay. Ecclesiastical appointments were frequently sold for huge amounts of money. Several popes of the period had become notorious for their corruption. Unlike the popes of today, they sent armies into battle, hunted game, and generally neglected their religious duties in favor of worldly pleasures. During the second half of the 15th century, Italian churchmen in particular had begun to acquire a reputation for unabashed worldliness and cynicism, qualities that were very much in evidence in Rodrigo Borgia's behavior as a prince of the Church.

The Roman Catholic church that Rodrigo and his family were to use as a springboard for their ambitions possessed very little of the moral and spiritual authority that it had known several centuries earlier. In fact, the popes' having reduced Christianity to a commercial undertaking would eventually cost the papacy much of its credibility. The conduct of churchmen like Rodrigo would eventually provoke a cataclysmic reaction from devout and independent-minded Catholics. Early in the 16th century the resolute defiance of the papacy shown by a German theologian named Martin Luther would signal the beginning of the period of religious, political, and social upheaval known as the Reformation. Christendom would find itself divided, never again to know the unity that had characterized the first 1,500 years of its existence.

Rodrigo's decision to name his son Cesare had much to do with the fact that the boy was born at the height of a cultural period later known as the Renaissance. (This is a French term meaning rebirth.) The Renaissance, which generated new forms of consciousness that found expression in some of the greatest literary and artistic achievements of all time, originated in Italy and was characterized by a revival of interest in the literature, philosophy, and politics of ancient Greece and Rome. The Renaissance is generally considered to have begun early in the 14th century.

At the beginning of the Renaissance, Italy was much more fragmented than it would be in Cesare's time. The country consisted of numerous independent city-states, some of which had adopted democratic forms of government. This trend did not last very long, however. Wars raged continually throughout Italy during the 14th century and the first half of the 15th, as the various cities vied with one another for commercial domination. Many cities fell into the hands of powerful tyrants, several of whom were condottieri. Then, the larger states began to absorb the smaller ones. Dictatorships replaced the fragile democracies, and despotism became prevalent. By the end of the 15th century most of the territory in the Italian peninsula was controlled by the five most powerful states: the republic of Florence, the duchy of Milan, the republic of Venice, the Papal States (a vast stretch of central and northeastern Italy over which the papacy exercised temporal and spiritual authority), and Naples (then a Spanish kingdom covering the southern half of the peninsula).

A woodcut from a 16th-century edition of the *Decameron*, a collection of stories by Giovanni Boccaccio, shows Florentines fleeing an outbreak of plague. An early masterpiece of Renaissance Italian literature, the *Decameron* was greatly influenced by humanism, the secular philosophy that formed the basis of the education received by Cesare and many of his peers.

The leaders of Italy's city-states fell into five categories: feudal lords with hereditary rights to their territories; noble appointees to military command who had repaid their employers by enslaving them; the condottieri, who often used the fees they commanded to finance their own wars of conquest; the wealthy despots who ruled Italy's republics; and those nobles designated imperial vicars of the Holy Roman Empire. The almost continuous conflict among these states was the background against which the Renaissance unfolded and grew to its majestic maturity.

The first of the great Renaissance Italian writers was the poet Francesco Petrarca, or Petrarch, who lived from 1304 to 1374. His originality stemmed from the fact that much of his work contained sentiments derived from the Greek and Latin classics, which he studied for many years. The second great figure of the Italian literary Renaissance was Giovanni Boccaccio, whose masterpiece, *Decameron*, consists of 100 stories supposedly recounted by young Florentines who have fled to the countryside following an outbreak of plague in the city. Boccaccio flouted convention by making jokes about the clergy and celebrating sexuality with an exuberance that distinguished him from his predecessors. In general, the work of the major Renaissance Italian writers of the 15th century exhibited a passion for pre-Christian, pagan culture and represented a rejection of Christian teachings and morality.

Although much Renaissance Italian literature continues to enjoy a wide readership, it is the great art generated during the Italian Renaissance that stands as the period's greatest achievement. The most famous Italian painter of the 14th century was Giotto, whose work was so true to life that, according to one story, one of his friends attempted to brush a fly from a surface upon which Giotto was working only to discover that it had been drawn there by the artist.

Despite the indisputable brilliance of much 14th-century Italian painting, it was the 15th century that saw the greatest achievements in Renaissance Italian art. The first great figure of this period was

Madonna and Child with Two Angels, **by Fra Filippo Lippi, whose work marked the beginning of a tradition of depicting the psychological state of subjects in paintings.**

Tommaso di Giovanni di Simone Guidi, known as Masaccio, who is acknowledged as a major innovator in the area of perspective. The revolution that Masaccio had initiated was to be continued by Fra Filippo Lippi and Sandro Botticelli.

The greatest Italian painter of the late 15th and early 16th centuries was Leonardo da Vinci. An outstanding painter, Leonardo was also a sculptor, musician, architect, mathematician, scientist, and philosopher. His strong belief that it was the artist's duty to look deeply into the secrets of nature is apparent in all his work. It has been said of Leonardo that "nothing that he touched but turned into a

ALINARI/ART RESOURCE

A detail from *Birth of Venus*, by Sandro Botticelli. Although most Renaissance Italian paintings reflect the aesthetic sensibilities of the wealthy religious and political leaders who commissioned them, many pieces — including Botticelli's — have a timeless quality that transcends the circumstances under which they were executed.

thing of eternal beauty."

Inseparably linked with the Renaissance in art was the intellectual movement known as humanism, which was eventually to influence all of Europe. Humanism represented a radical departure from medieval ways of thinking, which viewed the world exclusively in relation to God. Humanists viewed the world strictly in human terms.

Although by the middle of the 15th century humanist scholars were lecturing at many Italian universities alongside equally learned but more traditionally-minded clergymen, the relationship between humanism and the Church remained uneasy. Many clerics distrusted humanists because they studied pre-Christian, pagan cultures.

Under the influence of humanism, Italy's leaders adopted the values of the ancient Roman ruling classes. They cultivated the quality of *virtù* (virtue), which combined skill and courage. With this quality they tried to overcome the unpredictable force known as *fortuna* (fortune) and thus acquire *fama* (fame). They came to revere the pronouncements of humanists such as Leon Battista Alberti, who said, "A man can do anything if he wills." As a result, socially prominent young Italians such as Cesare were brought up to believe that they could make of the world whatever they chose. By the same token, their humanist tutors, as self-appointed guardians of high culture, were often dismissive of the poor, mocking their ignorance and stupidity.

One of the humanists' favorite concepts was "the dignity of man." What the humanists meant by this, however, was the dignity of a few men — the princes who could afford to employ them. In 1438 a humanist named Matteo Palmieri wrote in his book, *On Civil Life*, "If people from the lowest orders of society earn just enough to keep going from day to day, then that suffices." Antonio Ivani, another leading humanist, suggested that servants and workers should either be decently fed or properly paid because "being from the lowest orders, to get enough food for their stomachs is almost their only concern."

The yawning gulf that separated the ignorant multitude from the privileged few was widening as the 15th century drew to a close. Throughout Italy, increasing amounts of land began to pass into increasingly fewer hands. Not only had the monasteries expanded their holdings, but great merchants and wealthy noblemen had begun to buy so much land that they virtually enslaved the peasantry. The prominent and propertied gradually turned away from active involvement in trade and instead they acquired a taste for living off the interest from their investments. They cultivated a sedate lifestyle.

The beautiful palaces, churches, and mansions built during the Renaissance were financed by Italy's ruling families and the princes of the Church with the profits they made as absentee landlords. Many noblemen added to their fortunes by taking commissions as condottieri, hiring out their military skills. One such captain, Federigo da Montefeltro, spent the tremendous sum of 200,000 ducats on the construction of a palace when the average workman of the time earned just 16 ducats a year.

In this elitist culture that so highly valued ap-

ALINARI/ART RESOURCE

A detail from a 14th-century Italian fresco shows peasants laboring in the fields. Although much of his wealth derived from the sale of crops and goods produced by the peasants who worked the Church's estates, Cesare, like many other members of his class, looked down upon the lower orders of society.

pearance and affectation, the princes of the Church could not afford to lack the qualities that had brought their secular counterparts to prominence. Rodrigo Borgia was no exception to this rule. Although wealthy, successful, and respected, he remained ambitious. He regarded his prominence in the College of Cardinals, the assembly that provided the only major constitutional check on the powers of the pope, as a stepping-stone to higher office. Rodrigo Borgia had hoped to gain the papacy for himself ever since his uncle, Cardinal Alfonso de Borgia, had been elected to the papacy as Calixtus III in 1455.

Thus it was that Rodrigo continued to seek promotion while Cesare graduated from the nursery to his first encounter, at about age five, with the rigors of the humanist schoolroom. Cesare and his younger brother Juan, who was born in 1476, spent their early years in a household fit for princes, maintained at Rodrigo's expense. Cesare especially would prove to be his father's son. In fact, before we can understand Cesare we must understand his father. Cesare came to prominence only because his father was famous and powerful. He was groomed for greatness only because his accession to greatness was assured. Thus the story of the Borgias begins

Gonzaga Family and Court, by Andrea Mantegna, is one of the many Renaissance Italian paintings that, in the opinion of some critics, reflect the ordered and austere tastes of the aristocrats and high-ranking churchmen who commissioned them.

A painting by Sano di Pietro portrays Pope Calixtus III as the protector of the city of Siena. The people of Siena commissioned the painting in 1456 — the year in which Calixtus appointed Cesare's father, Rodrigo, to the cardinalate.

with Alfonso de Borgia, the Spanish churchman who arrived in Rome, the "Eternal City" of Catholicism, in 1445 and proceeded to make it his own.

When Alfonso came to Rome, the city had barely begun to recover from years of neglect. Between 1305 and 1378 the popes had been absent from the city and the papacy had become a plaything of European monarchs. This situation had resulted from the eruption, in 1302, of a bitter dispute between Pope Boniface VIII and the king of France. The sub-

Rodrigo Borgia's uncle, Pope Calixtus III (at left, enthroned beneath canopy) elevates Enea Sylvio Piccolomini (kneeling before Calixtus) to the cardinalate. Shortly after his election to the papacy as Pope Pius II in 1458, Piccolomini reconfirmed Rodrigo as vice-chancellor of the Church.

sequent election of a French pope had led to the removal of the papal court to Avignon, a city in southern France, in 1305.

During the period of exile, Rome suffered a dramatic deterioration from splendor to squalor. Writing in the mid-14th century, Petrarch described it as "the most malodorous of cities, the sink of iniquity, the cesspit of the world." The affairs of the papacy did not return to anything resembling normality until 1417, when delegates to a general council of the Church elected a new pope, Martin V, who entered Rome in 1421 and set about rebuilding the papacy's prestige and finances.

Martin did his best to beautify the city, but this was no easy undertaking. His administration faced hostility from the Roman people and from the two most prominent Roman baronial families, the Orsinis and the Colonnas. Gang warfare, robbery, assassination, and rape were everyday events in Rome throughout Martin's reign.

Martin's successor, Pope Eugenius IV, fared little better. A commentator writing during his reign described Rome and the surrounding regions: "A territory ravaged by war, the towns depopulated and in ruins, the fields laid waste, the roads infested with brigands. . . . Many impoverished citizens have been sold as slaves; many have died of starvation in prisons." This situation was all too familiar to Romans when Alfonso de Borgia arrived in the Eternal City.

Alfonso lived quietly in a palace next to Santi Quattro Coronati, the church where he was cardinal-priest. By 1449 he had attracted many of his relatives to Rome, all eager to seek advancement within the Church. Among these ambitious men was Rodrigo, Alphonso's nephew, who, according to contemporary accounts, had a certain style that set him apart from other Borgias. As his tutor described him: "He is well-formed and speaks with honeyed eloquence. His attraction for beautiful women and the manner in which he excites them — and they fall in love with him — is quite remarkable. He attracts them more powerfully than a magnet does iron."

Shortly after his election to the papacy as Calixtus

III, Alfonso, considering how best to bring his family into the higher echelons of the Church, announced his intention to appoint two of his nephews — Rodrigo Borgia and Luis Juan de Mila — to the cardinalate. The other cardinals were stunned. Not only were the nominees young (Rodrigo was 25) and barely finished with their studies, but they had no real claim to preferment except through kinship with Calixtus.

What the cardinals resented even more, however, was the prospect of two more hogs at the gilded trough. Much of a cardinal's income derived from his share of a set portion of the Church's revenues that went specifically to the Sacred College. The more cardinals there were, the less money each made from this source. An additional problem was that the papacy's income tended to be erratic at this point in the Church's history.

Ever since the period of the Avignonese exile, the popes had been increasingly forced to rely on their "temporal income" — the revenues from the Papal States. Much of their "spiritual income" — revenues from territories outside the Papal States — had been signed away to the European powers, which had secured financial concessions from the papacy by means of intimidation.

The rulers of the cities of the Papal States generally held power as papal vicars. Although they held authority in the pope's name and were supposed to pay him annual dues, they rarely lived up to their obligations. The popes nevertheless managed to continue to derive substantial revenue from the Papal States. Any pope who had the political will to campaign against rebellious vicars stood to augment the Church's income and authority.

For this reason, many of Italy's leading families sought to secure for their sons a career in the Church. Since only cardinals were eligible for the papacy, the cardinalate was the ecclesiastical rank at which they aimed their offspring. In proposing his nephews for such office, Calixtus was following a time-honored, albeit somewhat dishonorable, tradition within the Church.

Duly appointed cardinal in 1456, Rodrigo proved

GIRAUDON/ART RESOURCE

A 15th-century Italian painting shows knights conducting a tournament, one of the many activities in which the young Cesare Borgia was encouraged to engage to improve his physical prowess.

to be very capable. He went as papal legate to Ancona, a town in the Papal States that had failed to pay its dues. There, he reasserted the Church's control and began to acquire a reputation as a competent administrator.

His nephew's successes convinced Calixtus that he had chosen well. He made Rodrigo a captain in the papal army, president of the Church's high court, and vice-chancellor of the Church. Other family members received a variety of appointments and, consequently, attracted hordes of their friends.

Following Calixtus's death in 1458, the cardinals gathered to choose a new pope. At first Rodrigo backed the leading French candidate, Cardinal d'Estouteville. He changed his mind, however, when approached by the leading Italian candidate, Cardinal Enea Sylvio Piccolomini, who suggested to the 28-year-old Spaniard that d'Estouteville, if elected, would not keep his promise to retain Rodrigo in the vice-chancellorship. Rodrigo declared for Enea at a point in the voting when the Frenchman was convinced he had the advantage. This dangerous but decisive move tipped the balance against the French faction. Piccolomini became pope, taking the name Pius II.

Rodrigo fared well under Pius and continued to make a name for himself as a gifted vice-chancellor. He also continued to cultivate the lifestyle of a Renaissance prince, channeling the profits from his benefices into the construction of a magnificent palace, one of the most ostentatious in Rome. In 1471, when Pius died, Rodrigo was selected to officiate at the coronation of Pius's successor, Sixtus IV.

In 1472 Rodrigo went as papal ambassador to his native Spain, where he granted to Ferdinand of Aragon and Isabella of Castile the papal dispensation that allowed them to marry despite the fact that they were closely related. During this visit, Rodrigo established a relationship with Ferdinand that was to be of occasional assistance to the Borgias for the rest of the century.

When Rodrigo returned to Rome in 1473, he began to expend much time and energy on cultivating the friendship of the new pope. Sixtus, in fact, was the kind of pope with whom Rodrigo felt comfortable. Both men considered rank an asset worthy of investment in one's family. Sixtus acted in character, therefore, when, in 1481, he declared Rodrigo's illegitimate son, Cesare, eligible to hold all ecclesiastical offices except the cardinalate. Rodrigo thought little of this limitation at the time since one did not have to be a cardinal to make a lot of money. By 1484 Cesare, just nine years old, had acquired nine benefices. The revenues from these appointments went toward his upkeep and education.

Cesare's first tutors introduced him to the study of Greek and Latin, thus laying the foundations for a humanist education. Intensive study of the works of the ancient Roman orator Cicero enabled Cesare to make speeches in Latin. From the writings of Julius Caesar, Tacitus, Livy, Herodotus, and Thucydides he gained an understanding of the history and politics of the ancient world. As the heroes of the distant past came to life in the pages of the classical authors, Cesare began to absorb their elitist and authoritarian values. This was the heart of

Lorenzo de' Medici, under whose despotic but enlightened rule the republic of Florence became one of the most powerful and prosperous states in Italy, renowned as a center of commerce, learning, and art. It was to Lorenzo's son Giuliano de' Medici that Machiavelli dedicated *The Prince*.

the humanist experience, and it was to people like Cesare, members of Italy's ruling classes, that humanism addressed itself.

In accordance with the educational ideals of the day, Cesare was also required to improve his physical prowess. He learned to run, jump, ride, and hunt. In these activities, too, he displayed the competitiveness that was to distinguish him for the rest of his life. In 1489, at age 14, he left Rome to attend the University of Perugia. There he studied both canon (church) and civil law.

In that same year, Cesare acquired another important appointment. He was made bishop-elect of Pamplona, a diocese in Spain. He would only become bishop of Pamplona once he had been ordained. In the meantime, as bishop-elect, he was still entitled to the considerable salary that went with the position.

In the fall of 1491 Cesare transferred to the university at the Florentine city of Pisa. This move was not made strictly on academic grounds. The university may have boasted one of the best jurists of the period, a scholar named Filippo Decio, but to Rodrigo Borgia the most important consideration was that one of Cesare's fellow students there would be Giovanni de' Medici, son of the Florentine ruler known as Lorenzo the Magnificent. Florence was a wealthy city-state whose friendship Rodrigo considered extremely valuable.

As it turned out, Cesare alienated Giovanni. Rodrigo had provided his son with a household and servants, and the extravagance of Cesare's lifestyle dismayed the other scholars. Although wealthy themselves, they found that they could not compete with Cesare. Giovanni's chancellor reported to Lorenzo that neither he nor Giovanni relished the thought of inviting Cesare to dinner. He bemoaned the fact that Cesare had "come [to Pisa] so well provided with tapestries and silver that our not having anything to equal it has left us a little perplexed."

To make matters worse, it became apparent that Cesare was not only wealthier than any of the other students, he was much cleverer too. Even the historian Paolo Giovio, who hated the Borgias, con-

Following his election to the papacy as Alexander VI in 1492, Rodrigo Borgia became even more notorious for corruption and immorality than he had been as a cardinal. Such was his political acumen, however, that within six years of his accession the Church's power and influence in Europe had increased substantially.

ceded that Cesare was a brilliant student. Of Cesare's performance in debates he wrote: "Cesare so profited from his studies that, with radiant intellect, he discussed in a learned manner the questions put to him in both canon and civil law."

While Cesare had thus been proving his intellectual worth, Rodrigo had been improving his own chances in the race for the papacy. Amassing appointments, consolidating his Spanish connections, expanding his household, and further beautifying his palace, Rodrigo continued to lead a spectacularly worldly existence. When Pope Innocent VIII fell ill in March 1492, Rodrigo immediately began to maneuver for the succession.

On August 6, 1492, two weeks after Innocent's death, 25 cardinals gathered to elect a new pope. Cesare was in Siena at the time, preparing to participate in an important horse race. Despite his devotion to sport, however, he was unable to give the race his undivided attention. The fortunes of the Borgias were at stake in this election.

Rodrigo soon emerged as the leading candidate of the Milanese cardinals. The spokesman for the Milanese interest, Cardinal Ascanio Sforza, swung his faction's votes firmly behind Rodrigo because the wily Borgia had offered him the vice-chancellorship that would become vacant if he were elected.

On August 11, 1492, crowds waiting outside the Vatican were informed that Rodrigo Borgia had been elected pope and had taken the name Alexander VI. That same afternoon a messenger brought the news to Cesare in Siena, who left for Pisa immediately, there to await his father's instructions. The gifted and arrogant 17-year-old rightly suspected that he would be called upon to put to practical use everything he had ever learned. His father was now spiritual leader of all Christendom and absolute overlord of the Papal States. He would undoubtedly demand much of his children.

Had the cardinals of the Church and the princes of Italy gained a glimpse of the future that day, they might well have trembled. Cesare Borgia had arrived at the threshold of a career that was to prove short —and horrifying.

> *It was during the age of the despots that the conditions of the Renaissance were evolved, and that the Renaissance itself assumed a definite character in Italy. Under tyrannies, in the midst of intrigues, wars and revolutions, the peculiar individuality of the Italians obtained its ultimate development.*
> —JOHN ADDINGTON SYMONDS
> British historian

2

From Sanctity to Scourge

The fact that the Borgia dynasty had well and truly arrived was soon evident to the Roman barons. The family coat of arms, which showed a bull upon a golden ground, was visible everywhere at Alexander's coronation. Workmen erected an effigy of this beast, symbolic of pride and aggression, before the Church of San Marco. The Borgia bull also appeared on the pope's personal banner.

While few doubted Alexander's strength of character, the direction in which he might propel the Church remained the subject of dispute. One commentator of the time explained the division of opinion: "Many believe that he will hold office with great majesty and ceremony, since His Holiness desires both fame and glory: and to do this he will be the father of all and maintain peace. Many think the opposite: that to dominate everything he will be a scheming Pope."

Those who expected the worst turned out to have been right. Within a month of the election, Alexander appointed Cesare archbishop of Valencia, a

Either Caesar or nothing.
—Cesare Borgia's motto

Alexander VI at prayer, as portrayed by Pinturicchio. The picture is a detail from one of the many frescoes that Alexander commissioned Pinturicchio to paint throughout the Borgia apartments in the Vatican.

city in Spain. Two months later, an ambassador to the Vatican wrote that "not even ten papacies would suffice to content this horde of relations." However, that same ambassador could not help but be impressed when he visited Cesare in March 1493. He wrote: "Cesare Borgia possesses both genius and charm. He has the breeding of a son of a great prince; above all, he is lively, merry, and fond of society. Being modest, he bears himself much better than does his brother [Juan]."

Along with his brother Juan and his sister, Lucrezia (who was born in 1480), Cesare was soon made aware of the part the Borgia children would play in their father's plans. Early in 1493 ambassadors to the Vatican heard rumors that Juan was to be made captain general of the Church and Cesare a cardinal. In February Lucrezia was betrothed to Giovanni Sforza, lord of Pesaro. This match was transparently political, since Giovanni was a nephew of Cardinal Ascanio Sforza (the prelate whose faction's votes had been decisive in Alexander's election) and of Ludovico Sforza, who had

Cesare's sister, Lucrezia Borgia. In 1500 Cesare had Lucrezia's second husband, Alfonso, duke of Bisceglie, murdered for having attempted to secure papal support for Spain at a time when Cesare favored closer relations with the French.

THE BETTMANN ARCHIVE

A portrait of Cesare by Raphael, one of the masters of Italian Renaissance art.

been de facto ruler of the duchy of Milan since 1481, when he usurped power from his weak and ineffectual nephew Gian Galeazzo Sforza, the rightful duke of Milan.

The only obstacle to Ludovico's plans was Gian Galeazzo's wife, Isabella d'Aragona, who realized that Ludovico would not remain content indefinitely with his unofficial status and that he was determined to make himself duke. The fact that Gian Galeazzo did not object to being completely overshadowed by Ludovico failed to deter Isabella from seeking to protect her husband's rights and privileges. Isabella's grandfather, King Ferrante of Naples, who greatly valued his kingdom's association with Milan, was deeply worried by Ludovico's maneuverings. Another factor that disturbed Ferrante

Italian explorer Christopher Columbus takes leave of his royal patrons, the Spanish monarchs Ferdinand of Aragon and Isabella of Castile in 1492. By approving the Spanish claim to the New World, Alexander hoped to ally the Borgias with the royal house of Aragon.

was the status of Naples in relation to the papacy. Since the kings of Naples were traditionally approved in their positions by the pope, the prospect of the Borgias favoring the Milanese pretender and thus endangering his granddaughter's position alarmed Ferrante.

Unfortunately for Ferrante, the French monarchy had a rival claim to the kingdom. Even as Ferrante worried about developments in Rome and Milan, King Charles VIII of France was considering the conquest of Naples. And Ludovico Sforza was thinking of inviting Charles to invade Italy and depose Ferrante. The fact that an Italian ruler had no qualms about encouraging a foreign power to shatter the peace of the peninsula so as to gain a state for himself is a perfect example of the corruption then plaguing Italian politics.

Alexander backtracked on his alliance with Ludovico just a few days after Giovanni and Lucrezia's wedding. On June 19, 1493, Alexander was warned that Ferdinand of Aragon and Isabella of Castile would support Ferrante in the event of a French invasion. Alexander also learned that, in exchange for papal approval of Spanish claims to the New World, which had been discovered by the Italian explorer Christopher Columbus in 1492, Ferdinand would propose the marriage of his own cousin, Maria Enriquez, and Cesare's younger brother, Juan Borgia, duke of Gandia, thus allying the Borgias with the house of Aragon by kinship.

In September 1493 Alexander set about making Cesare a cardinal. Cardinal Giuliano della Rovere, one of Alexander's most implacable enemies, exploded with rage when he heard the news of Cesare's nomination. Cesare, who was away from Rome when the election results were announced, made his official entry into the Eternal City as cardinal of Valencia on October 17. A few days later, he received a letter from Charles VIII, who asked Cesare to use his influence with Alexander to secure a cardinal's hat for his chief minister.

Charles's request demonstrated his eagerness to gain Alexander's favor in hopes of persuading him

Intent upon conquering Naples and gaining papal support for his venture, King Charles VIII of France invaded Italy in 1494. The skillful diplomacy that Alexander displayed in neutralizing the French threat to the independence of the papacy and the peace of Italy provided Cesare with a valuable lesson in statecraft.

to support the French claim to Naples. Although some of his advisers had questioned the feasibility of an invasion, Charles remained adamant. In fact, his resolve had begun to frighten Ludovico Sforza, who now doubted that he would gain very much from actively encouraging foreign intervention in Italian affairs.

As French intentions became clearer, Alexander, recognizing that any army marching on Naples would pass through the Church's territories, set about inspecting the fortifications of the cities in the Papal States. Much to Cesare's delight, he also took great care to keep his son informed of the options available to the papacy and briefed him on the issues at stake.

Alexander's problems were further aggravated when Ferrante died in January 1494. Charles VIII immediately informed the pope that if he favored Alfonso, Ferrante's son and heir, he would seek to have the pope deposed. Confronted with the necessity of choosing between the Franco-Milanese bloc and the Neapolitans, Alexander decided that his interests would best be served by a continued Spanish presence in Naples. Della Rovere and the Sforzas responded by criticizing Alexander's decision and continuing their intrigues.

On March 17, 1494, Charles VIII announced that he would invade Italy. On April 23 della Rovere left his fortress at Ostia in the hands of the Colonna family and fled to France. Alfonso was crowned king of Naples in May. Later that same month, Cesare's younger brother Jofré was married to Sancia, a granddaughter of Ferrante. Alexander and his family, now completely aligned with Naples, recognized the risks involved, since they had known that Charles would consider a marriage alliance between the Borgias and Naples an insult to France.

The alliance with Naples was the Borgias' only real asset. The loyalty of many papal cities was in question, Venice had declared neutrality, and Milan was, of course, committed to a pro-French policy. The forces available to the papacy were minimal, and the Neapolitan armies, although led by gifted condottieri, would not suffice to defeat the French.

The papal and Neapolitan commanders were still finalizing their defensive plans when Charles's army crossed into Italy on September 3, 1494. The fact that the Italian people were disenchanted with their rulers became obvious as city after city opened its gates to Charles and his 30,000 men. Cries of "*Francia! Francia!*" ("France! France!") resounded in marketplace and cathedral square.

On November 23, 1494, Charles entered Florence unopposed. He was welcomed by the merchants of the city, who had overthrown the de' Medici oligarchy in disgust at Piero de' Medici's having surrendered the republic's fortresses without a fight.

Alexander still refused to desert the Neapolitan cause. To the duke of Ferrara, with tears in his eyes, he said: "Although I am a Spaniard, not the less for that do I love Italy, nor do I wish to see Italy in the hands of anyone but Italians." Meanwhile, the French were advancing fast. They entered the Papal States in late November and arrived beneath the walls of Castel Sant'Angelo, the Vatican fortress, on December 19.

At this point Alexander decided that he might best

The armies of Charles VIII enter Florence on November 23, 1494. Many Italians, disaffected with the ruling elite, welcomed the invading French as liberators.

neutralize Charles's military advantage by exploiting the French king's notorious stupidity, gullibility, and ignorance. Accordingly, he instructed the cardinals and the allied commanders to admit Charles to Rome. On December 31, while the population of the Eternal City stared slack-jawed at Charles's army, Alexander and Cesare beat a hasty retreat to Castel Sant'Angelo through a tunnel that led from the Vatican to the fortress.

Even as the French raped, robbed, and butchered the helpless Roman people, Alexander and Cesare laid their plans. When a section of Castel Sant'Angelo's outworks collapsed just as Charles was bringing up his artillery, Alexander surrendered immediately. He agreed to Charles's demand that Cesare be handed over as a hostage for the duration of the Naples campaign. Alexander also granted the French army free passage through the Papal States and announced an amnesty for the churchmen and nobles who had rebelled against the papacy and supported France. In return, Charles promised to obey the pope, to acknowledge both his political and spiritual authority, and to act as his protector.

Alexander dazzled the Frenchman with the splendor of life at the papal court. The rituals of protocol, the lavish hospitality, and the spectacular entertainments were beyond all Charles's previous experience. The fabulous ostentation first amazed and then seduced him. Italian rulers loved to display material evidence of their importance — and the impressionable Charles was struck almost speechless by the opulence.

Although Alexander had not addressed the most important issue — the French claim to Naples — Charles made no mention of his previous calls for reform of the Church or of his threat to have the pope deposed. Accompanied by Cesare, he departed for Naples on January 28, 1495. Alexander's seeming lack of concern over Cesare's predicament became understandable just two days later. Cesare, following a plan that he and his father had devised shortly after surrendering Sant'Angelo, escaped from Charles's clutches disguised as a royal groom.

Even as Charles marched south to claim Naples (where the cowardly Alfonso had abdicated, leaving the kingdom to his son Ferrantino), Alexander worked to establish an anti-French alliance between the papacy, Venice, Milan, Spain, and the Holy Roman Empire, which came to be known as the Holy League. Cesare, though heavily involved in the negotiations, found time to get even with some of the troops that Charles had left to garrison Rome. On April 1 a gang of 2,000 Spaniards waylaid a number of Swiss pikemen, killed 24 of them, and beat up the rest.

While the blood of Swiss mercenaries ran in the gutters of Rome, Charles and his army were antagonizing the entire population of Naples. According to a Venetian observer, "the French were boorish, unclean, and unprincipled people. They mistreated the women, showing no respect toward them, then they robbed them. [Nevertheless] they spend much time in church at their prayers." Discipline in the French forces collapsed beneath an excess of women and wine. Finally, in May 1495, Charles woke up to the threat represented by the new alliance and set off on the long journey back to France. He intended to stop in Rome to have his claim to Naples approved by the pope, but Alexander had other ideas on the subject. With the creation of the Holy League, the papacy had greatly enhanced its own security. As the armies of the Holy League came together in northern Italy, Charles quickened the pace of his march, hoping to leave the peninsula before his enemies were sufficiently organized to offer battle. His efforts to avoid a fight were in vain, however. The Italian armies intercepted the French near Fornovo, a town on the Taro River, on July 5, 1495. A bloody but indecisive battle ensued. The Italians captured much of the booty that the French had taken earlier in the campaign, but were unable to achieve the crushing victory for which they had hoped. Charles —who showed great courage during the battle—and his lieutenants were able to disengage their forces in good order and continue their march back to France.

Alexander's handling of the French intervention

ALINARI/ART RESOURCE

The triumphal arch built by King Alfonso I of Naples was one of the many majestic monuments past which the victorious armies of France paraded upon their entry into the city in 1495.

had been of immense value to Cesare. From it he gained a deeper understanding of the uses of power and of how to turn a disadvantage into a source of success. He had also learned that it was possible to take precautions against the blows of fortune.

The ability to take such precautions was to become one of Cesare's most distinctive attributes. It was something that Machiavelli not only admired in Cesare but considered essential in any ruler.

At one point in *The Prince*, Machiavelli wrote, "So as not to rule out our free will, I believe that it is probably true that fortune is the arbiter of half the things we do, leaving the other half or so to be controlled by ourselves." Machiavelli compared fortune with "one of those violent rivers which, when they are enraged, flood the plains, tear down trees and buildings, wash soil from one place to deposit it in another. Everyone flees before them, everybody yields to their impetus, there is no possibility of resistance. Yet although such is their nature, it does not follow that when they are flowing quietly one cannot take precautions, constructing dykes and embankments so that when the river is in flood they would keep to one channel or their impetus be less wild and dangerous."

To any but the Borgias, the situation in Rome during the French intervention would have seemed impossible. Alexander, however, had turned a disaster into triumph by correctly perceiving his opponent's true nature and using it to deflect him. In so doing, his tactics were truly Machiavellian. Fortune had thrust the French upon Alexander, but the pope's imagination and willpower proved more than equal to the situation.

The French invasion made Cesare keenly aware of the weaknesses of the Italian system. The speed at which the city-states had fallen before the French advance, the rulers who imagined themselves omnipotent but who caved in when confronted with the need to show some courage — these factors allowed Cesare to take the measure of the men he would have to oppose in order to advance the fortunes of the papacy and the Borgias alike.

Throughout the winter of 1495–96, Alexander

48

consolidated his gains on the political front while leading a life of unabashed worldliness. He lavished much affection upon his latest mistress, the beautiful Giulia Farnese, who was 43 years his junior. Alexander's enjoyment of life and the fact that he did not hide it gave the Borgias a reputation for scandal in addition to the one they already had as masters of intrigue.

Cesare now lived in the Vatican as palace cardinal. In April 1496 Lucrezia abandoned Pesaro and her loveless marriage to Giovanni Sforza and returned to Rome. There, her father and Cesare showed her the extravagant devotion that often characterized relationships within the Borgia family. In fact, many of their contemporaries believed that Lucrezia indulged in incest with both Alexander and Cesare. Suspicions that this was the case remain quite common today. It must be remembered, however, that much of the Borgia legend was contrived by their enemies. And yet, given that Alexander, Lucrezia, and Cesare were products of their time, the possibility that they were incestuous cannot be discounted. The practice was certainly not unknown among the Italian upper classes during this period.

In May 1496 Jofré and Sancia arrived in Rome from Naples. Alexander chose to use the occasion of their entry into the city to demonstrate the extent of his international preeminence. The prince and princess of a few thousand acres of southern Italy were formally greeted by the entire Sacred College, 200 of the Vatican guards, and the ambassadors of Spain, Milan, Naples, Venice, and the Holy Roman Empire.

Since Jofré was but a boy of 15 and Sancia a mature woman, it came as no surprise when rumors began to circulate that she and the stunningly handsome Cesare were having an affair. However, this distraction was no consolation to Cesare. His brother Juan — who had always been Alexander's favorite son — had just returned from Spain, and his three-year absence turned out to have changed nothing.

Cesare soon discovered that he had not displaced his brother in his father's affections. He became

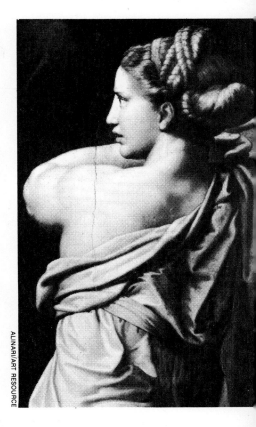

Giulia Farnese, whom British historian Sarah Bradford has described as "the last passion of Rodrigo Borgia's passionate life," was Rodrigo's mistress both before and after his election to the papacy. The pope's relationship with Giulia, who was 43 years his junior, scandalized all Italy.

extremely jealous when Alexander appointed Juan captain general of the Church and sent him out as second-in-command to Guidobaldo da Montefeltro, duke of Urbino, on a campaign against the Orsinis. (This predatory baronial clan had continued to defy the pope's authority in the region around Rome known as the Campagna, and Alexander had not forgotten their defection to the French in 1494.)

Juan's initial efforts in the Campagna were disastrous, and led to Guidobaldo's capture by the Orsinis at the Battle of Soriano on January 24, 1497. Juan redeemed himself at the siege of Ostia in March, though the taking of the fortress there could not have been accomplished without the genius of Gonzalo Fernández de Córdoba, the Spanish general who had taken command of the papal armies following Guidobaldo's capture. At the victory celebrations in Rome, Alexander granted Juan and de Córdoba equal honors, which the proud Spaniard and the assembled diplomats considered somewhat tactless.

Cesare's resentment of this situation was not purely the result of jealousy. It seemed dangerous to Cesare that his father should honor an incompetent young captain who had fled the field in his

The young man on horseback portrayed in this detail from Pinturicchio's *The Disputation of St. Catherine* is believed to be Cesare's brother Juan Borgia, who was assassinated in 1497. Although many people suspected Cesare of having ordered Juan's murder, this was never proven to be true.

first battle and later taken credit for victory away from the man who deserved it. Although at the time Cesare was not yet tending toward independence from his father, it is almost certain that he thought it inadvisable that Alexander should allow his affection for Juan to blind him to the young man's shortcomings and damage the family's standing.

In June 1497 Alexander appointed Cesare papal legate to Naples for the coronation of Ferrantino's successor, King Federigo, thus continuing his policy of cultivating the Neapolitan connection and gradually severing all ties with Milan. Alexander realized that the failure of the recent French intervention did not preclude the possibility of similar incursions in the future. The French king's cousin, Louis, duke of Orléans, had a valid claim to Milan, and Alexander did not intend to waste time and effort on staying allied with a duchy that was guaranteed to fall should the French decide to invade.

At around the time that Cesare gained his legateship, Alexander granted Juan hereditary rights to the cities of Terracina and Pontecorvo, thus giving his family a direct stake in the papal territories. Alexander's move, to the outrage of clerics and laymen alike, perpetuated the decadent and much-

Every day in Rome one finds men murdered, four or five a night, bishops, prelates, and others.
—PAOLO CAPELLO
Venetian diplomat,
writing in 1498

51

abused system of papal appointments. Cesare, however, cared nothing for the discomfiture of the pope's opponents. What concerned him was the fact that Juan had thus become the prime target of anti-Borgia sentiment.

On June 16, 1497, while trawling a stretch of the Tiber River near the Church of Santa Maria del Popolo, a fisherman hauled in what felt like a heavy catch and discovered that he had netted a corpse. The gorgeous clothes in which the body was dressed, and the handful of gold pieces in the cadaver's waist purse, left the fisherman in no doubt as to the identity of his catch. He knew that papal troops had been scouring the city for two days, searching for the missing Juan Borgia.

Alexander was shattered by the death of his favorite son. And yet, within just three days of the disaster he was once more in control of his emotions and said to an assembly of cardinals and diplomats: "The duke of Gandia is dead. His death has given us the greatest sorrow, and no greater pain than this could we suffer, because we loved him above all things, and esteemed not more the Papacy nor anything else. Rather, had we seven papacies we would give them all to have the Duke alive again. God has done this perhaps for some sin of ours, and not because the Duke deserved such a cruel death; nor do we know who killed him and threw him into the Tiber."

People pointed the finger of accusation in many directions. Suspicion fell upon such enemies of the Borgias as Giovanni Sforza, Cardinal Ascanio Sforza (who resented the fact that the Borgias had sided with Naples during the French invasion), Guidobaldo da Montefeltro (who was still smarting at Alexander's refusal to ransom him from the Orsinis following his capture at Soriano), and Jofré Borgia, who naturally resented the fact that his wife, Sancia, had been having an affair with Juan after ending one with Cesare.

The Orsinis, however, were the most plausible culprits. It had been their strongholds that Juan (with substantial assistance from de Córdoba) had assaulted the previous winter. And it was common knowledge that they thought Alexander responsible for the death of their former leader, Virginio Orsini, in January 1497.

During the first few weeks of 1498, Alexander and Cesare began to revise their plans for the dynasty. Juan's death and Jofré's immaturity meant that Cesare was now the most powerful weapon in Alexander's family arsenal. Father and son decided that Cesare should take the unprecedented step of renouncing the cardinalate. Cesare would then be free to marry. The marriage, of course, was to be as politically advantageous as possible.

It was around this time that Rome began to buzz with rumors that Cesare had engineered Juan's death. Although some historians have dismissed these charges as typical examples of anti-Borgia

After Juan Borgia's murder, Pope Alexander VI decided that Cesare could best aid the family's dynastic interests by renouncing the cardinalate and making a politically useful marriage. Upper-class Europe was shocked by the strong-arm tactics Alexander employed to free his son from his religious duties.

propaganda, others have suggested that Juan's death represented Cesare's first political assassination. Juan's arrogance, incompetence, and provocative behavior undoubtedly placed the family at risk. Where cunning, pretense, and calculation ought to have been employed, Juan had been content to flaunt the prominence that he had gained but did not really deserve. He might well have proved worse than useless to the Borgias had he lived. It is not improbable that Cesare became convinced that Juan's death would be no loss to the Borgias, while his continued existence would probably have been disastrous.

It was, therefore, as both the Borgia heir-apparent and, in some people's estimation, a probable murderer, that Cesare announced his intention to abandon the cardinalate. Unfortunately for Cesare, he found himself speaking to a half-empty house on this occasion: most of the cardinals had left the city rather than face having to approve a request which, according to Church law, no cardinal had a right to make.

Incensed by their attitudes, Alexander sent messengers to the resort towns where the cardinals had taken up residence. They were told to return to the Eternal City "because matters were to be debated concerning the good of the Church and Christianity." At the second consistory, or meeting of pope and cardinals, which was held on August 23, 1498, all resistance crumbled. Two days later the Venetian ambassador to the Vatican wrote: "The Pope, with all the cardinals' votes, has given license that the Cardinal of Valencia, son of the Pope, could put off the hat and make himself a soldier and get himself a wife."

The news from Rome scandalized the ruling classes throughout Italy, Spain, and France. Subsequent revelations of the papal scheming that had preceded the strange turn of events at the Vatican disturbed them even more.

Following the death of Charles VIII in April 1498, his successor, Louis XII, had begun to make overtures to Alexander. He needed the pontiff's blessing on his two most important projects — securing a di-

The ruin of Italy is confirmed . . . given the plans which Alexander and Cesare have made: but many believe the Holy Spirit has no part in them.

—GIAN LUCIDO CATTANEO
Mantuan diplomat, writing in 1498 of the negotiations between the Borgias and France

vorce and invading Italy. He was eager to be rid of his wife, Jeanne de France, so as to marry Charles's widow, Anne of Brittany. Also, as Charles's successor, Louis had inherited Charles's claim to Naples, and could now contemplate making himself lord of southern Italy as well as ruler of Milan.

Alexander resigned himself to the prospect of another French invasion. Despite the fact that Spain was the only power capable of standing up to Louis in the event of French interference in Naples, the pope had no intention of putting the papacy in debt to Ferdinand and Isabella. Alexander therefore decided to start playing the two nations off against each other.

To achieve this, he wanted to secure the marriage of Cesare and Carlotta of Aragon, a legitimate daughter of King Federigo of Naples. Since Carlotta lived in France and was officially under French protection, such a match would mean that Cesare would be marrying into the Spanish royal house and would also become an ally of France — Spain's traditional enemy. Alexander persuaded Louis to support his ideas, much to the annoyance of Ferdinand, who had no wish to see Spain made a Borgia dependency in the event that the Neapolitan branch of the house of Aragon should ever find itself with a claim to the succession in Ferdinand's kingdom. Federigo, who was becoming increasingly disturbed by the pope's seemingly inexhaustible appetite for intrigue, had no desire to see Carlotta ensnared by the Borgias. He realized, however, that he could not afford to alienate them completely, and decided that offering his illegitimate son Alfonso, duke of Bisceglie, as a husband to Lucrezia might serve to keep relations between the papacy and Naples harmonious and to convince the pope that marriage between Cesare and Carlotta was still a possibility. Alfonso and Lucrezia were married in the Vatican on July 21, 1498.

The secret agreement between the Borgias and Louis XII revealed the extent to which Alexander, in order to further his own dynastic interests, had committed himself to the French cause. Cesare was to be made duke of Valence and Diois; he would also

In 1498 King Louis XII of France negotiated an agreement with Pope Alexander VI whereby Cesare was to be admitted into the ranks of the French nobility. In 1499 Louis arranged Cesare's marriage to Charlotte d'Albret, sister of Jean d'Albret, king of Navarre.

be granted an army of 2,000 heavy cavalry that would be maintained at Louis's expense. He would receive an annual grant of 20,000 gold francs, the lordship of the city of Asti, and membership in the chivalric Order of St. Michael.

By mid-summer 1498 it had become apparent that Alexander, in promising Louis his divorce and thus aligning the interests of the Borgias with those of France, had not only abandoned Milan but forsaken Naples. Federigo's continuing reluctance to countenance the prospect of marriage between Cesare and Carlotta — in which he was supported by Ferdinand of Aragon — had convinced the pope that there was now little to be gained from the Neapolitan connection.

While Alexander negotiated with the French, Cesare worked extremely hard to improve his physical condition and to prepare himself for the trials of a military career. As if to symbolize his change of status, Cesare commissioned the crafting of a gorgeous parade sword, decorated not only with the Borgia family's traditional heraldic insignia but also with inscriptions that referred to the life and times of his famous namesake, Julius Caesar.

It was now apparent to everyone that it was upon Cesare that Alexander was pinning his hopes of advancing the Borgias. Alexander recognized that the dynasty's fortunes would not be well served were they to remain solely dependent upon the Church. Alexander intended to use his influence as pope to secure for his family a foothold in secular politics whence it could, in turn, exert influence on his successors. Alexander realized that his family's prominence was entirely the result of his own nepotism, and that the power it enjoyed could not be expected to last very long following his death. He was keenly aware of the fact that the power of the papacy, while substantial, lacked the ingredient that gave secular power its long-term preservation — hereditary tenure. Ultimately, the power of the papacy was only as strong as the pope who wielded it. Since the papacy was always at the mercy of the secular powers and could not itself be secularized, the only way in which it could possibly function as a force for stability both within and beyond its own borders would be in alliance with a secular power whose interests were identical to its own. For Alexander, establishing Cesare as a secular prince was the first step in this revolutionary direction.

Under the terms of the deal that Alexander had struck with Louis, Cesare was to go to France to be married to Carlotta. Eager to make a good impression on the French, Cesare and his father embarked upon a tremendous spending spree, making the best possible use of the 200,000 ducats that the pope had raised by appropriating the worldly goods of several hundred Roman Jews and confiscating the property of a heretical Spanish bishop.

From the moment of his arrival at the southern French seaport of Marseilles in October 1498, Cesare's personal magnificence and the trappings of wealth that adorned both his horses and his henchmen astounded the French. Despite the problems of protocol raised by the fact that there was, understandably, nothing in the code of etiquette regarding the correct way in which to receive the son of a pope, Cesare made a magnificent entry into the royal castle at Chinon on December 18, 1498.

An illustration from Duc de Berry's *Book of Hours* depicting workers toiling outside a castle in Renaissance France. Cesare traveled to France in 1498 in order to marry the daughter of France's King Louis XII. Although she refused to marry him, Cesare stayed on in France to cement the alliance between the Borgia family and the powerful French court.

Cesare and Louis quickly established a warm relationship, and the young Italian soon became the center of attention at the French court. Within weeks Cesare had so impressed the king's men that they forgave him his initial swaggering and bravado. Painfully aware of the fact that he had not come to France simply to win a popularity contest, Cesare then began to suspect that circumstances might prevent him from furthering his secular career. Carlotta had refused to contemplate marrying him, and her attitude did not change even when she learned that Louis was considering sending her into exile as punishment for her obstinacy.

Despite this setback, Cesare reasoned that he would do well to stay on in France. Louis was as eager to take Milan as Charles VIII had been to conquer Naples, and achieving a formal alliance with the papacy had become an integral part of his Italian policy. Cesare also recognized that it was only with the benefit of a solid agreement with France that Alexander could hope to resist the ever-increasing pressure to which he was being subjected by the anti-French factions in Rome.

In the wake of the Carlotta fiasco, Louis made every effort to find a suitable bride for his Italian guest. On May 10, 1499, he signed a contract approving the marriage of Cesare Borgia and Charlotte d'Albret, daughter of Alain d'Albret, duke of Guyenne. The document stated that the king consented "[being] duly informed of the great and worthy services which Don Cesare de Bourgia, Duke of Valentinois, has rendered to him and to his crown, and hoping that the aforesaid Duke, his relatives, friends, and allies will render them unto him in the future, and likewise for the conquest of the kingdom of Naples and the duchy of Milan." The fact that Cesare actually liked Charlotte was an ironic but unimportant twist to the marriage's more significant political implications.

Throughout the early summer of 1499, as Louis concentrated his armies north of the Alps, his enemies in Italy began to take to their heels. Cardinal Ascanio Sforza left Rome for Milan, where his brother Ludovico was frantically trying to work out how best he might survive the coming onslaught. Lucrezia's husband, Alfonso, sought the protection of the Colonnas. Sancia deserted Jofré and returned to her native Naples, thus providing further proof of the extent to which Alexander had alienated the house of Aragon.

On October 6, 1499, with Cesare figuring prominently in his entourage, Louis XII made a magnificent entry into Milan, where he discovered that Ludovico Sforza had saved not only his own life but also the family jewels. The mighty Sforza treasure chests, with their special locks designed by Leonardo da Vinci, stood empty. Their owner had fled to safety in Austria.

Louis's aggravation did not last very long. He considered the splendors of the Milanese ducal palaces sufficient compensation for his warlike exertions. Plus, he could boast ownership of Ludovico's fabulous stables, adorned with frescoes of his horses, and Leonardo's *Last Supper*, a remarkable painting that still graces the Milanese monastery of Santa Maria della Grazie. Louis undoubtedly found the Italian penchant for self-glorification somewhat ex-

Illustration depicting Francesco Sforza and his *condottieri* in classical Roman garb. Although ruling families such as the Sforzas were great patrons of the arts, they usually exacted a price from the artists they supported — subject matter was often dictated by the artists' sponsors, who sometimes insisted on themes that presented themselves and their families in a heroic light.

travagant compared to the more reserved sensibilities that characterized life at his own court. Ludovico Sforza's palaces contained dazzling evidence that in Renaissance Italy life at court centered exclusively upon the prince.

In his book *Power and Imagination: City-States in Renaissance Italy*, historian Lauro Martines wrote, "Never before had Italian ruling groups owned so much faith in their ability to control the perceived reality of the surrounding world." Ludovico Sforza, for example, commissioned Leonardo to create a colossal bronze statue of his father, Francesco Sforza. But because of the duchy's financial difficulties the project ground to a halt when Leonardo had done no more than complete the massive clay model that was to be used for the casting. The model was destroyed by Ludovico's enemies after his downfall in 1500, an action which, according to Martines, demonstrates that "art in our terms was hated propaganda in theirs."

Another practitioner of lordly narcissism was Francesco Gonzaga, fourth marquis of Mantua. Toward the end of his life he was confined to his suite by illness and consoled himself by keeping his favorite pets in the room with him. Surrounded by pedigree greyhounds and prized falcons, he sat amid his finest furnishings and gazed at magnificent paintings of his beautiful horses. He was waited upon by servants who had shaved their heads to match his own, which he kept bald. Thus, the heads of his attendants reflected his features. His image was visible upon the men who served him.

The behavior of men like Francesco Sforza and Francesco Gonzaga clearly demonstrates that, by the end of the 15th century, the egocentricity of Italy's princes had become a state of mind that considered everything in the natural world its own. Writing in 1491, Ludovico Sforza's wife, Beatrice d'Este, described a day she spent at the family hunting grounds: "Every day I am out on horseback with dogs and never do we return, the lord my consort and I, without our having had infinite pleasures falconing. . . . There are so many hares, leaping up from all sides, that sometimes we know not which

way to turn to have our pleasure, for the eye is incapable of seeing all that which our desire craves and which the country offers us of its animals."

Another means whereby a prince might flaunt his power was patronage of artists. When Lorenzo de' Medici estimated his family's expenditures between 1434 and 1471, he made no attempt to draw up separate accounts for architectural and artistic commissions and payments of taxes and charitable contributions. In his eyes, all such disbursements had served the same purpose — they had added to the grandeur of the de' Medici dynasty.

Many important 15th-century paintings embody the organized rationality idealized by the men who commissioned them. For instance, one critic has said of Piero della Francesca's portraits of the da Montefeltro family that they show "man in complete control of nature." Andrea Mantegna's *Madonna of the Stonecutters* is another example. In this way artists in Renaissance Italy were necessarily propagandists for the values of the rulers who employed

Christ Giving Keys to St. Peter, by Perugino. The emphasis on perspective and the predominance of urban contexts that characterize much of Perugino's work reflect the preoccupation with organizing urban space that was common among the upper-class Italians who commissioned such pieces.

61

Mantegna's *Madonna of the Stonecutters*. The slabs and columns that the stonecutters are crafting in the background are typical of the architecture of ancient Rome, whose culture Cesare and his peers idealized.

them, even when the subject of their paintings was ostensibly religious. And it was to the ducal city of just such a domineering Renaissance ruler that Cesare had come, on October 6, 1499, at the head of a company of French knights.

For all his visions of nobility and his inflated sense of self-esteem, Ludovico Sforza had not been prepared to stand and fight in defense of Milan. Once again, Cesare was confronted with evidence of the weakness of Italy's princes and the fragility and disunity brought about by the way in which they exercised their power. Although it may seem improbable that the concept of political unity could have concerned Cesare at a time when he and his father were allied with the invading power, it was at this point that Cesare began to consider the possibility of bringing peace to the Romagna, the most unruly province of the Papal States. Alexander and Cesare now hoped to make use of Louis XII's support to secure an Italian state for Cesare.

The Romagna had long been a thorn in the papacy's side. The papal vicars who ruled the Romagnol cities had consistently flouted the pope's authority. Alexander realized that if Cesare could reunite the province he would have created a state of immense strategic importance. He would also have made himself one of the leading princes of Italy.

With such a goal in mind, Alexander's nepotism stood revealed as the cornerstone of his policy for the Papal States. He had calculated that no one but a son could better serve his purpose, which was to rid the Papal States of the turbulent vicars who never obeyed him and who often allied themselves with foreign invaders or with Italian states bent upon eroding the Church's supremacy. Alexander intended to entrust to his son the formidable task of uniting the Romagna and ruling it in his own right and as a true defender of the Church.

Alexander and Cesare recognized that they could not hope to achieve very much without the support of the king of France. Florence and Venice regarded the Romagna as falling within their own spheres of influence and would only make concessions once persuaded that Louis had an interest in the venture.

Louis duly agreed to aid the pope in the recovery of the Romagna and declared that he had "constituted our dear and well-loved cousin Cesare Borgia, duke of Valentinois, as our lieutenant." Much to the dismay of the Romagnol rulers (whom Alexander had already decreed both dispossessed and excommunicated), Cesare was to command not only the papal armies but also 300 French knights and 4,000 Swiss and Gascon infantrymen that Louis had promised from his own forces.

On December 17, 1499, Cesare's army reached the city of Forlì, ruled at that time by a cunning and ruthless noblewoman named Caterina Sforza. Caterina soon found that she had little upon which to depend except the dubious loyalty of her subjects

Caterina Sforza, ruler of Forlì, whom Cesare dispossessed in January 1500. Notorious for her cruelty, Caterina greatly enjoyed witnessing the atrocities to which Cesare's French troops subjected the townspeople of Forlì.

The castle of Rocca di Forlì, one of the most formidable fortresses in the Papal States, was captured by Cesare in January 1500, during the early stages of his first campaign to restore the Church's authority and power in the region.

and the walls of her citadel, the Rocca di Forlì. Her disappointment at her subjects' immediate capitulation to Cesare and his commanders was partially assuaged by the barbaric treatment that the French troops inflicted upon the townspeople of Forlì.

The fortress fell on January 12, 1500, following a concerted artillery bombardment that Cesare directed in person. He took Caterina prisoner and set out for Cesena, the next city on his itinerary. On January 26 Cesare was informed that Ludovico Sforza had left Austria with 8,000 Swiss and 500 Burgundian troops and was marching on Milan. Cesare's French contingent departed for Milan immediately, leaving him with only 1,000 infantry and 500 horsemen. He abandoned his plans for the capture of Pesaro, Rimini, and Faenza, and returned to Rome.

Cesare's triumphant entry into the Eternal City on February 26, 1500, made a disturbing impression on the ambassadors to the papal court. Gone was the flamboyant young man with whom they had all been familiar. In his place they now beheld an austere and aloof politician and soldier. Cesare wore a plain robe of black velvet that set off his features more dramatically than had his previous colorful silks. From this point onward, black was to emerge as Cesare's chosen color.

At the victory parade that marked his return to Rome, Cesare sought to project himself as a second Caesar and to make it apparent that he had learned to survive in the secular environment since abandoning the cardinalate. He had gained the confidence of the king of France and of the powerful, intelligent men who served him. He had acquired a beautiful and socially prominent wife and several valuable lordships in France.

Cesare had also learned a great deal about warfare from the French. Unlike many of the French commanders, however, he had exhibited the caution and flexibility that distinguish the useful general from the glory seeker whose victories inflict almost as much damage upon his own forces as they do upon the enemy. At Forlì, Cesare had made careful use of artillery so as to minimize casualties among the assault troops. The excesses committed by the French forces had convinced him not only of the importance of discipline but also that he would need to recruit his own troops in the future. In fact, Cesare had learned in a matter of months more about soldiering and politics than many men learn in a lifetime. At age 24, he was a force with which to be reckoned.

Louis XII rides at the head of a company of knights. The French king provided Cesare with 2,300 soldiers for his campaign in the Romagna in 1503.

GIRAUDON/ART RESOURCE

A 15th-century painting of St. Mark's Cathedral in Venice. Venetian rulers consistently exercised their formidable military and political power in attempts to absorb the northernmost provinces of the Papal States into their sphere of influence, giving Cesare and Alexander cause for concern.

It is not surprising that such a man watched events in Italy during the spring of 1500 with a measure of frustration. Despite having been appointed captain general of the Church, Cesare was in no position to continue his campaigns in the Romagna. The papal armies simply would not suffice for such a major expedition. Further ventures would still require French support, and Louis's armies had been tied up in Lombardy since February, seeking to dislodge Ludovico Sforza from Milan. (Ludovico had returned to Milan on February 5, 1500, following a successful campaign against the French garrisons in Lombardy.)

Cesare and Alexander were eager to recommence operations in the Romagna for several reasons. They could not afford to settle for the partial control that the family now exercised in the region. Any hereditary state that Cesare carved out for himself within the papal domains would have to be secure. Only as hereditary captain general of the Church and overlord of the Romagna would Cesare stand a chance of weathering such disasters as the election of an unfriendly pope and military pressure from the powerful republic of Venice.

In April 1500, following Ludovico's defeat and capture by the French (who had managed to mount a successful counterattack against the Milanese), the Borgias opened a concerted diplomatic offensive. Alexander's ambassadors were instructed to dangle the bait of the Neapolitan crown before Louis and to promise the Venetians papal support for a crusade against the Turks on condition that Venice immediately withdraw its protection from the papal vicariates of Rimini and Faenza. However, neither Louis nor the Venetians showed much enthusiasm for Alexander's proposals, and negotiations dragged on into the summer.

In July 1500 Cesare's reputation for ruthlessness became even greater. The murder of Alfonso Bisceglie, Lucrezia's husband, demonstrated that even members of the Borgia family were not safe from Cesare's machinations.

Severely wounded on July 15 by would-be assassins who were probably hired by the Orsinis, Alfonso had been nursed back to health by Lucrezia and Sancia. By mid-August many people suspected Cesare had been involved in the attempt on the duke's life. Alfonso, as a member of the Neapolitan branch of the house of Aragon, had continued to support the Spanish claim to Naples. Throughout the entire period of Cesare's visit to France, both Alfonso and Sancia had done their best to dissuade Alexander from pursuing pro-French policies.

Cesare's resentment of this threat to his ambitions finally translated into action on August 18, 1500. His henchman, da Corella, burst into the apartments in the section of the Vatican known as the Torre Borgia, where Alfonso was convalescing, and arrested Alfonso's uncle and the Neapolitan ambassador. He then informed Lucrezia and Sancia that only the pope's intercession would secure the

> *Cesare's brutalities were always calculated: there is not one single recorded instance of his committing an act of violence which he would have considered unnecessary or from which he did not stand to gain.*
> —SARAH BRADFORD
> British historian

Ego sum Papa.

A 16th-century cartoon portrays Alexander as an agent of the Devil. When the pope died, Machiavelli, even though he had admired Alexander's political abilities, could not resist the temptation to moralize: "The soul of the glorious Alexander," he wrote, "was now borne among the choir of the blessed. Dancing in attendance were his three devoted handmaidens: Cruelty, [Bribery], and Lechery."

prisoners' release. By the time the two women returned from speaking with Alexander, da Corella had suffocated Alfonso.

Alfonso's murder convinced many observers that Cesare had been responsible for the death of his brother Juan in 1497. Hatred of the Borgias became increasingly intense and widespread. As far as Cesare was concerned, however, the killing had not only stifled disaffection within the family but had also inspired fear in many other people and thus diminished the prospect of resistance to his ambitions.

Five days after Bisceglie's death, Cesare gained yet another victory. French envoys arrived in Rome and announced that Louis XII would grant Cesare the services of 2,300 troops for a campaign in the Romagna if the Borgias would promise to provide him with diplomatic and military assistance in his projected assault on Naples. By September the Borgias had managed to add to their existing advantages by reaching a working agreement with Venice. The republic abandoned Rimini and Faenza to whatever fate might await them at the hands of the Borgias.

On October 1, 1500, Cesare's 10,000-man army set out from Rome and began the long march to the Romagna. For the first time in his political career, Cesare was in supreme command of forces intended to reassert the papacy's authority in one of its most unruly provinces. Every Italian with an interest in politics now recognized that the Borgias were about to make their most determined bid for a dynastic and territorial supremacy that might one day make them masters of all Italy.

The ambassador from Mantua spoke for many of his contemporaries when he voiced his suspicion that "the pope plans to make [Cesare] great and king of Italy, if he can; nor do I dream, but all can be described and written down, and so that others will not think my brains are disordered, I will say no more."

The confusion sown by the Borgias since Alexander's accession to the Throne of St. Peter in 1492 had been greatly to their advantage. In playing off

France and Spain against each other and falling afoul of neither, they had enhanced the international prestige of the papacy. Alexander's capacity for deception and his son's capacity for ruthlessness were legendary. Cesare had become adept at charming those people whose interests coincided with his own and at disposing of those who threatened him. His personality had come to contain sophistication and savagery in equal proportions — a combination that Machiavelli considered essential in the ideal ruler.

In a chapter of *The Prince* entitled "How princes should honor their word," Machiavelli wrote: "You must understand, therefore, that there are two ways of fighting: by law or by force. The first way is natural to men, and the second to beasts. But as the first way often proves inadequate one must needs have recourse to the second. So a prince must understand how to make a nice use of the beast and the man."

In the same chapter of *The Prince* Machiavelli gave a disturbing assessment of the man from whom Cesare had learned much of his statecraft — Alexander. In Machiavelli's opinion, "Alexander VI never did anything, or thought of anything, other than deceiving men; and he always found victims for his deceptions. There never was a man capable of such convincing asseverations, or so ready to swear to the truth of something, who would honor his word less. Nonetheless his deceptions always had the result he intended, because he was past master in the art."

Such were the qualities that Cesare and Alexander were about to deploy in the fall of 1500. Sophistication and savagery were to characterize their actions in the months ahead to a greater extent than they ever had before. Alexander and Cesare hoped to lay the foundations of a new political order in Italy. If they could achieve the creation of a hereditary Borgia state strong enough to withstand all opposition and to dictate to the other states of Italy, then the peninsula's traditional internal discord and vulnerability to foreign invasion might yet be brought to an end.

Alexander VI was a stronger and a firmer man than his immediate predecessors. All considerations of religion and morality were subordinated by him with strict impartiality to policy: and his policy he restrained to two objects — the advancement of his family and the consolidation of the [papacy's] temporal power.
—JOHN ADDINGTON SYMONDS
19th-century historian

3

A Prince in Search of a People

Even as Cesare's army marched northward, his agents stirred up trouble in the first two cities targeted for assault. On October 10, 1500, Pandolfo Malatesta ceded Rimini to Cesare's representative. On October 11 most of the leading citizens of Pesaro marched at the forefront of a mob demanding the expulsion of the Sforzas, and by the following evening Giovanni Sforza was on his way to exile in Venice.

Cesare entered Pesaro in triumph on October 27, making a great impression on both the populace and the ambassadors from neighboring principalities. By the time Cesare entered Rimini on October 30, news of his victories was causing consternation throughout Italy. The Florentines were worried by the fact that several of Cesare's captains were Orsinis — allied by marriage with the exiled de' Medicis and dedicated to their reinstatement. Meanwhile, the rulers of Bologna knew they had displeased Cesare by supporting the continued rule of Faenza by Astorre Manfredi, whose vicariate Alexander had declared forfeit.

Cesare Borgia will be, if he lives, one of the first captains in Italy.
—PAOLO CAPELLO
Venetian diplomat, writing in 1500

In October 1500 Cesare embarked upon his second campaign to crush those rulers of cities in the Papal States who had refused to acknowledge the authority of the pope. Seven months later, Alexander appointed Cesare duke of the Romagna — one of the most important provinces in the Papal States.

ALINARI/ART RESOURCE

The Florentines' anxiety increased when it became apparent that Cesare's relationship with Louis XII would undermine the protection the city normally received from France. As Machiavelli reported, "Louis, with regard to the affairs of Italy, [held] the pope in higher esteem than any other Italian power."

French approval of papal policy implied approval of the papacy's chosen instrument — Cesare — and demonstrated that Alexander had made the Church a powerful contender for political supremacy in Italy. The Borgias were greatly aided by their foreknowledge of the Treaty of Granada, in which France and Spain agreed to divide Naples between them. With this treaty, Ferdinand of Aragon abandoned his Neapolitan relatives, leaving Louis free of the threat of Spanish intervention that had previously made him uneasy about pressing his claims in southern Italy.

Cesare was now convinced that he could pursue a course of action likely to disturb Florence without having to worry unduly about possible French opposition. The ever-increasing confidence that he now wore like a second suit of armor was dented, however, when Faenza put up a harder fight than anticipated. On November 26, with the resistance showing no sign of diminishing, Cesare left the condottiere Vitellozzo Vitelli in charge of a small blockading force and dispersed the rest of his army throughout the Romagna.

Following the arrival of French reinforcements in February 1501, Cesare prepared to resume the siege of Faenza. When the city capitulated on April 25, Cesare demonstrated his respect for Manfredi and his people by declining to stage an official entry. Having thus charmed Astorre Manfredi into taking service with him, Cesare went on to Bologna, where the ruling Bentivoglio family had already decided to come to terms with the Borgias. Paolo Orsini negotiated the agreement on Cesare's behalf, and approved the inclusion of a clause, suggested by Giovanni Bentivoglio, which stated that Giulio Orsini, Paolo Orsini, and Vitelli would guarantee to restrain Cesare from making assaults on Bolognese

territory in the future. This agreement was to have serious repercussions for both Cesare and the signatories at a later date. For the time being, however, consolidating Cesare's power was the paramount concern. On May 15, 1501, Alexander invested Cesare as duke of Romagna, thus confirming him in perpetual lordship over one of the most important provinces in the Papal States.

Cesare returned to Rome and discovered that his father had been busy during his absence. Alexander was preparing to dispossess the Colonnas, whose continued support for the Spanish cause in Naples had greatly annoyed him. The pope had also decided that it might be advisable to protect himself against possible French coercion and was, therefore, busy

The atrocities committed against Neapolitan civilians by German mercenaries during the French invasion of Naples in 1501 greatly disturbed Cesare, who was fighting for the French at that time. Unlike other military commanders of his day, Cesare disapproved of the mistreatment of civilians, although foreign troops under his command sometimes performed brutal acts.

supervising improvements to the fortifications of Castel Sant'Angelo.

Cesare left Rome to join the French on July 12. The campaign proved easy, the only serious fighting taking place at Capua. The bloodiness of the military engagement was greatly surpassed by the savagery of the subsequent sack of the city: Cesare was appalled by the wanton brutality of the German and Gascon infantry. When the French army marched into Naples on August 3, 1501, Cesare rode toward the front of the procession, in company with some of Louis's most important commanders.

Following Cesare's return from Naples in September 1501, he and Alexander set out to inspect the strongholds that the Colonnas and several other baronial families had ceded to the papacy.

By the fall of 1501 the Borgias were in a very strong, and quite unprecedented, position. For the first time in the history of the Church, most of the papal territories were in the hands of a single family. Of the principalities ceded by the Colonnas, Alexander had conferred the duchy of Nepi upon the infant Giovanni Borgia (whose paternity remains a mystery to this day) and the duchy of Sermoneta upon Rodrigo, Lucrezia's son by Alfonso Bisceglie. Cesare, already overlord of the Romagna, was now considering moving against the last pockets of resistance to the papacy in two other provinces of the Papal States — Umbria and the Marches. And Alexander was working to secure the northern borders of the Romagna against Venetian interference by arranging that Lucrezia be married to Alfonso d'Este, heir to the duchy of Ferrara — a small but strategically important city-state situated between Venice and the Romagna.

In December 1501 Ferrante, Sigismondo, and Ippolito d'Este journeyed to Rome from Ferrara on behalf of their brother Alfonso, Lucrezia's prospective third husband. Ippolito, acting as Alfonso's proxy, gave Lucrezia a gold wedding ring, thus sealing the marriage and linking the fortunes of the Borgias with those of the d'Estes, one of the most powerful ducal families in Italy.

Following Lucrezia's departure for Ferrara in Jan-

Alfonso d'Este, the Ferraran nobleman whom Lucrezia Borgia married in 1501. Alexander believed that a marriage alliance between the Borgias and the rulers of Ferrara, which was situated directly between the Papal States and the Venetian republic, was politically wise.

uary 1502, Alexander and Cesare withdrew from the public eye. Ambassadors to the Vatican began to find it increasingly difficult to secure an audience with either of them. One thing was certain: the Borgias would surprise everyone once they decided to make their move.

Finally, on June 4, 1502, the waiting was over. The ink was barely dry on the Venetian envoy's report that Cesare and Alexander were still haggling over projected military expenses when the Florentine city of Arezzo rebelled and prepared to open its gates to Vitelli. On the same day, the citizens of Pisa seceded from Florence, offering Cesare lordship of their city. On June 13 Cesare joined his army of 6,000 infantry and 700 men-at-arms at Spoleto. Many observers suspected that he probably intended to march upon Camerino and Senigallia, which were two of the most important towns in the Marches. But a few others remembered the recent rumor that Cesare might be about to move against Guidobaldo da Montefeltro, the duke of Urbino.

A respected condottiere and man of learning, the wealthy da Montefeltro, whose court was one of the most magnificent in Italy, had long hoped that he would never be forced to choose between his allegiance to the pope and his own desire for political independence and continued friendship with Florence. (The fact that Alexander had refused to ransom him from the Orsinis following his capture at the Battle of Soriano in 1497, thus forcing his wife to sell her jewels so as to regain his freedom had, not surprisingly, left him with little inclination to serve the Borgias in any capacity.) Now, with Borgia condottieri on the rampage in Florentine territory, da Montefeltro was placed in an awkward position. He delayed his response to Cesare's request that he send troops to Vitelli at Arezzo only to discover that Borgia troops from the Romagna were at his borders and Cesare himself at Cagli, just 20 miles away. Da Montefeltro had believed that Cesare was at Camerino, which was 100 miles distant.

Faced with Borgia soldiery bearing down upon Urbino from two directions and Cesare approaching from a third, da Montefeltro fled his duchy, barely

Guidobaldo da Montefeltro, duke of Urbino. Caught between his allegiance to the pope and his friendship with the city-state of Florence, da Montefeltro hesitated to support Cesare's forces in their occupation of the Florentine town of Arezzo, and was expelled from his duchy in 1502 as a result.

avoiding capture. Thus it was that without the direct support of a foreign power, acting on his own initiative, and commanding his own forces, the 27-year-old Cesare Borgia had dispossessed one of the most prominent rulers in Italy. The organizational brilliance and perfect timing that Cesare had displayed in executing this coup stunned both his allies and his opponents.

On June 24, 1502, three days after his triumphant entry into Urbino, Cesare granted an audience to Machiavelli and Francesco Soderini, bishop of Voltera. The two diplomats had been ordered to Urbino by the Florentine government at Cesare's request. Cesare had been determined to have his way with Machiavelli's paymasters ever since May 1501, when he had used the threat of force to extract from Florence both a treaty of friendship and a condottiere's commission. Describing his first impression of Cesare, Machiavelli wrote: "This Lord is truly splendid and magnificent, and in war there is no enterprise so great that it does not appear small to him; in the pursuit of both glory and lands he never rests nor recognizes fatigue or danger. He arrives in one place before it is known that he has left another; he is popular with his soldiers and he has collected the best men in Italy; these things make him victorious and formidable, particularly when added to perpetual good fortune."

In his negotiations with the Florentine diplomats, Cesare made his position chillingly clear: "I know well that you are prudent men and understand me; however, I will repeat what I said in a few words. I do not like [your] government and I cannot trust it. You must change it and give me guarantees of the observance of the promises you made me; otherwise you will soon realize that I do not intend to live in this way, and if you will not have me as a friend, you shall have me as an enemy."

At this point in the talks, Machiavelli returned to Florence to deliver Cesare's ultimatum to the ruling council there, leaving Soderini to cope as best he could alone. Soderini soon found himself up against a quality in Cesare that is often the mark of a prudent leader. He learned from various members of

Elisabetta da Montefeltro, whose husband, Guidobaldo, Cesare dispossessed in 1502. When Cesare further humiliated Guidobaldo by making his sexual impotence public knowledge, Elisabetta declared that she preferred to maintain a sisterly relationship with her husband rather than divorce him.

Cesare's household that "[Cesare] alone decides, and at the moment of action, so that his purpose cannot be known beforehand."

What the anxious Soderini failed to recognize was that Cesare was not simply seeking more territory. Several of Cesare's mercenary captains — Vitelli, the Orsinis, and Gian Paolo Baglioni — were lords of papal cities that had not yet formally acknowledged his authority. Cesare realized that their suspicions that he might one day seek to dispossess them could only have increased with the capture of Urbino. The situation was dangerous, and Cesare desperately wanted a working relationship with the Florentines, whose assistance would be useful should he be forced to suppress his subordinates. Freedom to move at will through Florentine territory, which bordered upon both the Romagna and Urbino, would greatly aid him in the event of a confrontation with his own condottieri.

Cesare became even more anxious following Louis XII's arrival in Milan at the end of July 1502. Many of Cesare's enemies, including da Montefeltro, flocked to the French king, begging Louis to abandon his alliance with the Borgias. When Louis spoke disapprovingly of the fact that Borgia commanders had disturbed the peace of Florence, Cesare had no choice but to make the required response. He threatened to march against Vitelli's lordship of Città di Castello unless Vitelli withdrew from Flor-

The da Montefeltro family's magnificent ducal palace at Urbino, which Cesare made his headquarters between June and September of 1502. Experts have estimated that its construction required that between 800 and 1,000 laborers work continuously during a period of 20 years.

entine territory. Since Florence was the only bone of contention between Louis and Cesare, no further concessions were required.

Although it appeared that the French king was humiliating the Borgias, Alexander and Cesare were actually negotiating with Louis, hammering out the details of a secret agreement that would have horrified the disgruntled condottieri had they known of its existence.

Early in August 1502 Alexander announced that the papacy would support Louis's impending campaign against the Spanish in Naples. (The Treaty of Granada had failed to keep the peace between Spain and France concerning the question of Naples, and the countries had been preparing to recommence military operations in that much-disputed territory since the early spring of 1502.) The pope also announced that he intended to confer upon Cesare the vicariates of Città di Castello and Perugia, thus dispossessing Vitelli and Gian Paolo Baglioni. On August 5 Cesare surprised everyone but Louis when he arrived in Milan and went straight to the French king's headquarters. His enemies began to realize that their attempts to drive a wedge between Cesare and the French had failed.

Cesare's standing with Louis was evidence of the special influence he now enjoyed. Machiavelli was moved to write, "The Duke [of Romagna] is not to be measured like other lords, who have only their titles, in respect to his state: but one must think of him as a new power in Italy."

At about this time Cesare demonstrated yet again the extent to which he outstripped many of his contemporaries in his scientific approach to the preservation of power. He hired the services of Leonardo da Vinci. This son of humble Florentine working people had acquired a fabulous reputation as a painter, sculptor, architect, physicist, and engineer. He worked for Cesare between the summer of 1502 and January 1503. Leonardo drew expert maps that Cesare and his commanders used in their campaigns. He produced town plans for Urbino and Cesena, and for Imola he devised an elaborate system of defenses.

Leonardo da Vinci, the famous painter, sculptor, architect, engineer, and scientist, worked for Cesare as a military engineer from the summer of 1502 to January 1503. Leonardo drew expert maps that Cesare and his commanders found useful while campaigning in the Papal States.

It is logical that one of the most brilliant political minds of the period should have enlisted the services of a great scientist like Leonardo. While his opponents took their power for granted and felt cheated when that very attitude was their downfall, Cesare took a scientific approach. Cesare's decision to have his commanders stir up trouble within the borders of the Florentine republic, which had long enjoyed the protection of his most powerful ally, must have seemed like political suicide to his opponents. Cesare must certainly have realized that the dispossessed vicars would try to turn Louis against him and capitalize on the French king's dis-

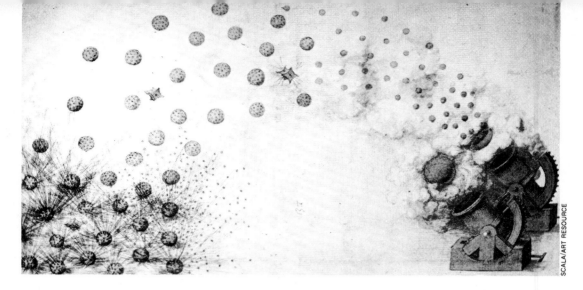

A sketch made by Leonardo da Vinci shows one of the many technologically innovative pieces of military equipment that he designed in the course of his long and prolific career — a siege mortar with a barrel capable of being swiveled and set at varying elevations.

pleasure. However, to counteract this anti-Borgia chorus Cesare had gone to Louis with an offer of direct military assistance and the continued support of the papacy. His opponents, however, having been dispossessed by Alexander, had nothing to offer Louis but themselves.

The way in which Cesare combined unpredictability with a genius for scheming and intrigue placed him in an unusual position within the Renaissance Italian political cosmos. As Machiavelli wrote, "I also believe that [the prince] who adapts his policy to the times prospers, and likewise that the one whose policy clashes with the demands of the times does not." It cannot be denied that Cesare was a leader who understood the turbulent times in which he lived.

Machiavelli said that in general there are two types of prince: the impulsive and passionate; and the cautious and dispassionate. Cesare, however, was a mixture of the two. Actions considered impulsive by his contemporaries were often later discovered to have been very carefully thought out beforehand. When he had time in which to lay plans, he rarely took the most obvious course.

Following his successful management of the crisis in Florence and his reconciliation with Louis, Cesare left for the Romagna in September 1502. There he immersed himself in a somewhat less frantic activity—the administration of his duchy.

Historians still differ as to just how Cesare governed the Romagna and what his subjects thought of the methods he employed. Most provincial populations in Italy at that time, when confronted with a new overlord, hoped for as few innovations as possible. Their main concerns were that their rights were preserved, that their local privileges were respected, a reasonable judicial system was kept in place, and that public order was maintained. Cesare, however, sought to achieve a compromise between preserving the status quo and making the Romagna a unified state.

Since he intended the duchy to become an effective power base, Cesare recognized the importance of imposing, as a first step toward political unity, some form of central government upon the region. Only in that way could he hope to avoid the factionalism that was often the downfall of other states. Cesare was, of course, aware that unity was not just uncommon in Italy at that time — it was generally considered to be virtually impossible. Visionaries like Machiavelli, however, had at least begun to plant the idea that unity would have to become a feature of Italian politics at some stage unless Italy was to remain fragmented and vulnerable.

Since the papal administration of the time was one of the best examples of effective civil government, it comes as no surprise that experienced and trustworthy churchmen eventually replaced the Spanish military governors installed throughout the Romagna in the early days of Cesare's reign. These men were trained bureaucrats who had been schooled in the greatest bureaucracy of the day — the Curia. They were administrators of a caliber previously unknown in the Romagna.

Cesare declared Cesena the capital of his new state and drew up plans for the construction of law courts, a university, and government offices. He also established a circuit court of appeals.

Another reason for Cesare's return to the Romagna was his intention to recruit troops from within the duchy for future campaigns. His first intended victims in the next round of fighting were the Bentivoglio family in Bologna, a city that Alexander had long desired to see returned to the Church's control. Since Giulio Orsini, Paolo Orsini,

This lord is very secretive, and I do not believe that what he is going to do is known to anybody but himself. And his chief secretaries have many times asserted to me that he does not reveal anything except when he orders it, and orders it when necessity compels and when it is to be done, and not otherwise.
—NICCOLÒ MACHIAVELLI
writing of Cesare Borgia in
December 1502

An illumination from a 14th-century Italian manuscript shows fortune, personified as a woman, passing judgment on those who seek her favors. Such personification occurs in the work of many Renaissance Italian writers, including Machiavelli, who described fortune as a woman to be beaten and coerced by aspiring rulers.

and Vitelli had previously promised Giovanni Bentivoglio that they would restrain Cesare from assaulting Bologna, Cesare's intentions amounted to a test of their loyalty. Cesare knew he was playing a dangerous game, and his father was growing extremely anxious.

In October 1502 news reached Alexander that just about every Italian petty lord hostile to the Borgias had attended a meeting convened by Cardinal Orsini at his castle at La Magione. At this conference, Gian Paolo Baglioni reminded his associates that between them they now commanded more troops than did Cesare. The time had come to strike, he said, before they found themselves "being devoured one by one."

The object of their hatred reacted with a serenity that dumbfounded his entourage. To Machiavelli (who was not reassured), Cesare declared: "Believe me that this situation is to my advantage, and they cannot show their hands at an hour when it will harm me less, nor can I, to fortify my position, wish for a thing that will be more useful to me; because this time I shall know against whom I have to defend myself, and I shall know my friends."

Machiavelli soon realized that he had underestimated the duke of Romagna. Over the next two weeks Cesare recruited 800 infantry from the region of the Romagna known as Val di Lamone and a further 6,000 foot soldiers from elsewhere in the duchy. With the vast amounts of money that the increasingly nervous Alexander had begun to send him, Cesare also engaged 2,000 Swiss and Gascon infantry—some of the best soldiers in Europe.

By the end of October Machiavelli had begun to share Cesare's increasing confidence: "The condition of this lord, since I have been here, has been ruled by nothing but his good fortune; the reason for which is the widespread belief that the King of France will assist him with troops and the Pope with finance, and another thing which is no less responsible for it; and this is that his enemies have delayed bearing down on him. Nor do I think that at this time they can any longer do him much harm, because he has garrisoned all the important places . . . and the fortresses he had provided for most efficiently; so that, as their ardor chills in the face of such arrangements, he can feel sufficiently secure to wait for reinforcements."

So accurately had Cesare gauged the weaknesses of his opponents that by the end of November 1502 their failure to move and his own incessant preparations had combined to bring about the complete collapse of the conspiracy. Realizing that they had miscalculated, the plotters rushed to come to terms with Cesare.

Cesare's apparent willingness to strike bargains with his disloyal lieutenants and to reinstate them in their previous positions of favor greatly confused many diplomats. Machiavelli, however, recalled a statement that Cesare had made back in October, when the conspirators had been sending him letters declaring their loyalty even as they staged a countercoup in Urbino: "Thus you see how they govern themselves: they keep up negotiations for an agreement, write me friendly letters, and today the lord Paolo is come to see me, and tomorrow the Cardinal [Orsini]; and thus they play games with me in their way. I, on the other hand, temporize, listen to every-

> *He, therefore, who finds it needful in his new authority to secure himself against foes, to acquire allies, to gain a point by force or fraud . . . could not discover an example more vigorous and blooming than that of Cesare.*
> —NICCOLÒ MACHIAVELLI

thing, and bide my time." Machiavelli realized that the game had yet to be played out to the end.

On December 10, 1502, Cesare and his army departed for Cesena. Alexander, initially encouraged by this sign of activity, became extremely annoyed when another 10 days elapsed without any further developments. He even went so far as to lose his temper in front of a Venetian messenger and referred to his son as a "son of a bitch, a whore, and a bastard."

On December 20 the French troops with Cesare's forces received orders to return to Milan. Cesare's intimates informed the ambassadors to his court that the duke of Romagna had dispensed with the French because they were simply too costly to maintain. Cesare then instructed his remaining commanders to march the army southward by a variety of routes and to rendezvous with him at Fano on the morning of December 31. Their ultimate objective would be Senigallia, where the former conspirators were now encamped. By that time, Cesare said, Oliverotto Eufreducci, lord of Fermo, would have entered the town on his behalf.

On December 28 Cesare heard from Eufreducci (whom he had known also to be involved in the plot against him) that the warden of Senigallia Castle had insisted on handing over the keys to the castle to Cesare himself. Cesare realized that this was simply a ruse concocted by the condottieri and that they hoped he would come to Senigallia with no company other than his immediate entourage. As Cesare had intended, the condottieri obviously had no idea of the size of his forces. When the condottieri finally beheld Cesare's army late in the afternoon of December 31, they realized they had been deceived.

Cesare's subsequent execution of two of the condottieri and his imprisonment of the other three amazed the princes of Italy. With this deed that Machiavelli thought "admirable," Cesare had surpassed all his previous coups. Louis described Cesare's success as "an act worthy of a Roman hero."

The man of the hour wasted little time in making political capital out of his triumph, proudly declar-

Alexander VI never did anything, or thought of anything, other than deceiving men; and he always found victims for his deceptions. There never was a man capable of such convincing asseverations, or so ready to swear to the truth of something, who would honor his word less.
—NICCOLÒ MACHIAVELLI
political philosopher

ing that he had disposed of men whom he considered "public pests . . . that swarm of troublesome insects who were ruining Italy." His statement, while undoubtedly containing elements of propaganda, should not be dismissed as mere self-promotion. Indeed, following his victory, Cesare said that he was "not a man to play the tyrant but to extinguish tyrants."

Cesare left Senigallia at noon on January 1, 1503, and made for Assisi. There, on January 7, he heard that two cities had already capitulated to his representatives — Fermo, the murdered Eufreducci's lordship, and Città di Castello. On January 27 Pandolfo Petrucci, the only conspirator whom Cesare considered an equal, agreed to quit Siena.

Cesare's assertion that he had claimed Siena for the Church did not convince Louis XII, however. Sienese territory bordered directly upon the Florentine republic, which was still officially under French protection. Louis instructed Alexander to convey his royal displeasure to Cesare, and the pope duly did so. Alexander was exasperated by Cesare's continuing preoccupation with affairs in the Romagna. The pope was desperate to finish off the Orsinis, and it was to Cesare, as captain general of the Church and commander of the papal armies, that the task would necessarily fall.

Cesare, however, was in no hurry to take further action against the Orsinis. Having executed Paolo and Francesco Orsini at Sarteano on January 18, he now felt that he had disposed of the only two members of that family who had directly opposed his interests. He had no quarrel with the other members of the clan and had even begun to consider them possible allies.

By April 1503 Alexander and Cesare's differing views of the Orsini question had become less of a problem. Matters of more importance were under discussion in the wake of events in Naples. Ferdinand of Spain's armies, led by de Córdoba, had defeated the French in two key battles. In May word arrived in Rome that de Córdoba had entered Naples in triumph. Alexander became convinced that France's power in Italy was now irreparably dam-

Machiavelli in retirement, as portrayed by Agnolo di Cosimo around 1525.

aged. Louis, however, was determined to send another army to Naples.

On August 8 Cesare summoned the French ambassadors and assured them that he would honor his previous commitment to support Louis's claim to the much-disputed kingdom of Naples. Despite the precariousness of the situation Cesare was convinced that he might still be able to follow an independent course once the French had passed through the Papal States on their way south. A few days later, however, disaster struck.

The summer of 1503 had been extraordinarily hot, and many more Romans than usual had died of *malaria perniciosa* — a dreadful fever borne by the millions of mosquitoes swarming in the marshes surrounding the city. This particular type of malaria caused violent vomiting and could raise a person's temperature to fatal levels in a matter of hours. On August 12 both Cesare and his father became sick.

Alexander died on August 18. Cesare, though greatly weakened and occasionally delirious, nevertheless managed to react to the situation with the instincts of a survivor. He sent da Corella, his henchman, and a squad of papal troops to ransack Alexander's apartments. The expedition yielded silver and jewels worth more than 300,000 ducats.

With Alexander's death there came to an end one of the most remarkable papal reigns in the history of the Roman Catholic church. In his book *The Borgias: The Rise and Fall of a Renaissance Dynasty*, British historian Michael Mallett pays tribute to Alexander: "He brought scandal on the Church by ostentatiously flouting the normal conventions of papal behavior, and yet as Pope his alliance was sought by the great powers of Europe, his army was the strongest in Italy, his capital a center of European diplomacy. As a result, on his death the prestige of the Papacy as a force in European politics had probably rarely been higher, but the prestige of the Pope as a spiritual leader can scarcely have been lower." It was left to Alexander's son to control the damage that would undoubtedly be done to the Borgias by Alexander's death.

The fact that he still had both money and troops did not console Cesare completely. He and Alexander had been working to bring Cesare to a position where he would have a good chance of defending his gains following the pope's death, and neither of them could have imagined that Cesare himself might be at death's door when his father died.

Cesare knew that he was facing a situation in which he stood to lose all that he had fought for. Without his father's support, he realized, he would be forced to fend for himself. He knew that he would have to fight back hard and fast, employing all his available resources. Every enemy the Borgias had ever made would be screaming for blood.

This 19th-century illustration shows Cesare and Alexander clutching at their chests and gasping for air. Because the two men became sick on the same day, some people believed, even many years after the Borgias' downfall, that Cesare and Alexander had been poisoned. In fact, they were stricken with malaria, a disease which proved fatal to Alexander, who died on August 18, 1503.

4

Mortal Wounds and Deathless Dreams

While Cesare appropriated his father's wealth and summoned reinforcements, da Montefeltro, the Orsinis, the Colonnas, the Baglionis, and many others prepared to avenge themselves on the Borgias. Florence and Venice aided the return of several of the dispossessed lords to their former estates. The situation deteriorated further when Cesare learned that French troops led by Francesco Gonzaga, the marquis of Mantua, were marching on Rome from the north and that Spanish forces under de Córdoba were marching on the city from the south.

On August 22, 1503, Cesare managed to regain the support of the Colonnas by promising them restoration of their lands. Without this agreement the Orsinis might have overwhelmed him when they entered the Eternal City with 2,000 troops later that same day. Outnumbered by the Borgia-Colonna coalition, the Orsinis withdrew to await a more favorable situation.

Meanwhile, the members of the College of Cardinals declared that there would be no election of a new pope until all warring factions, Cesare and his followers included, left the city. Although he considered this a reasonable request, Cesare remained determined to secure the election of a pope who

Better to die in the saddle than in bed.
—CESARE BORGIA

A sculpture of a winged lion soars above St. Mark's Square in Venice. When, in mid-August 1503, the rulers of Venice heard that Alexander had died of malaria and that Cesare was fighting to recover from the same affliction, they immediately ordered their armies to move against Cesare's strongholds in the Romagna.

An ambassador arriving at the Venetian court. Venice contested with Cesare for control of the Romagna.

would not be a threat to his interests. The Venetian ambassador assessed the situation accurately when he told his government that Cesare was "resolved by whatever means to make one of his own [people] Pope; since without that he sees himself losing everything."

Cesare's confidence increased when France and Spain began to vie for his support. On September 1, 1503, he signed a secret agreement with France, promising Louis the use of all his forces for the Naples campaign in return for the French king's agreement to support the Borgias in maintaining the estates they still held and in regaining those that they had recently lost. A few days later Cesare learned that news of his being "alive, well, and the friend of the King of France" had reached the Romagna just in time. The Vitelli, Sforza, da Montefeltro, Malatesta, and Baglioni families had already returned to their estates, but Cesena, Imola, and Faenza had remained loyal. News of his agreement with Louis had also persuaded Venice to cease meddling in the affairs of the Romagna and to offer Cesare its support.

On September 22 the Spanish cardinals, having done everything possible to prevent the election of a pope hostile to Cesare, managed to tip the voting in favor of Francesco Piccolomini, a nephew of Pius

II. Cesare knew that Francesco, as a Piccolomini, would not have forgotten that Cardinal Rodrigo Borgia had been largely instrumental in securing the election of Enea Sylvio, Piccolomini's uncle, in 1458.

Piccolomini's election as Pius III did not solve Cesare's problems. He realized that the new pope's advanced age — he was 63 — and infirmity would probably make for a very short reign. Anti-Borgia prelates like della Rovere, Raffaele Riario, and Giovanni Sforza would be more determined than ever to win the next election.

Cesare took some consolation from the fact that Pius wasted little time in opening a tough diplomatic offensive against Venice and the vicars who had taken advantage of Cesare's illness by returning to their former lordships. It soon became apparent, however, that the pope did not intend to back up his words with action. On September 26 Pius told the Venetian ambassador that "due to the pressure [that had been put on him] by the Spanish cardinals, [he] had been compelled to issue some briefs

CÆSAR BORGIA

In the immediate aftermath of Alexander's death, Cesare directed all his efforts toward securing the election of a pope who would not be a threat to his interests.

The Borgia castle at Nepi. In September 1503, following a declaration by the College of Cardinals that there would be no election for a successor to Alexander until all military forces had vacated Rome, Cesare and his followers withdrew to his castle.

in favor of Cesare Borgia, but [would] not give him any more help." Pius went on to say that "I do not intend to be a warlike, but a peace-loving Pope. . . . I wish no harm to [Cesare Borgia], for it is incumbent upon a Pope to show compassion to all, but I predict that by God's judgment, he must surely come to a bad end." In fact, Pius was secretly encouraging Cesare's enemies. Informed of the pontiff's true feelings by his still substantial network of spies, Cesare realized that the situation was critical. Deserted by the Spanish troops in his pay (whom de Córdoba had recalled to Naples upon learning of Cesare's agreement with France), Cesare now faced the prospect of a further reduction of his forces. Under the terms of the alliance with Louis, the bulk of his remaining soldiery would shortly join the French king for the campaign in Naples.

Cesare's enemies' forces now outnumbered his own, and hostile troops under Bartolomeo d'Alviano, a relative and partisan of the Orsini family, were already marching on Nepi, where Cesare had established his headquarters, from Urbino, Camerino, and Città di Castello. Faced with a choice between making a stand in the Romagna and returning to Rome, Cesare chose the latter course. He arrived in the city on October 3, riding at the head of 800 troops. His most powerful opponents within the Church, especially della Rovere, were enraged by his sudden reappearance. The pope had only allowed the young adventurer to return because Cesare had claimed that he was still extremely ill with malaria and was coming home to die.

On October 8 Pius confirmed Cesare as captain general of the Church, thus granting him as much official authority as he had enjoyed during his father's reign. Cesare immediately began to arrange for his return to the Romagna.

As the pope negotiated safe passage for Cesare's forces through Florence and the Orsini territories north of Rome, Cesare's position suddenly became untenable. D'Alviano and Gian Paolo Baglioni arrived in the Eternal City. Furious at having failed to catch Cesare at Nepi, they declared that they had come "to lay hands on the Duke, whom at all costs they desired to pursue to the death." Shortly thereafter, the Orsinis and Colonnas formed an alliance against Cesare.

Cesare was now defenseless. The French were too far away to be of any immediate assistance, and his few remaining troops were encamped several miles to the north of Rome. To make things worse, Pius was now seriously ill, and his doctors did not expect him to live very much longer.

On the evening of October 15, Cesare fled through the underground passage that linked the Vatican and Castel Sant'Angelo. On October 17 Pope Pius III breathed his last, much to the relief of Cesare, who realized that everyone in Rome, whether for the Borgias or against them, would now be more concerned with the election of Pius's successor than with the outcome of the struggle between the Borgias and their enemies.

Cesare used the respite to shore up his position.

And although there was a man in whom some spark seemed to show that he was ordained by God to redeem [Italy], nonetheless it was seen how afterwards, at the very height of his career, [he] was rejected by fortune.
—NICCOLÒ MACHIAVELLI
on Cesare Borgia

As was customary when the papal throne was vacant, all forces other than the papacy's were required to leave Rome. Thus, once the Orsinis and Colonnas had withdrawn from the Eternal City, the field was clear for Cesare to summon his own troops back to Rome.

Machiavelli merely noted that Cesare seemed to have regained a measure of his former confidence; he also suggested that only the election of a pope sympathetic to the Borgias could save the beleaguered dynasty from going under for good. All but two of Cesare's cities in the Romagna had surrendered to their former rulers. Cesare, reduced to being the duke of the Romagna in little more than name, realized that only if he were reconfirmed as captain general by Pius's successor could he hope to raise an army with which to regain his duchy.

On October 29 Cesare struck a deal with the leading Italian candidate, his old enemy della Rovere. In return for the votes of the Spanish cardinals, della Rovere promised to appoint Cesare captain general should he be elected.

On November 1, 1503, della Rovere emerged victorious and took the name Julius II. Within days of the election Cesare discovered that he had made one of the greatest mistakes of his life in believing della Rovere to be a man of his word. Della Rovere, who had coveted the papacy ever since he entered the Church, was not about to neglect his own interests by furthering those of the Borgias. Cesare continued to voice his hopes of regaining the Romagna "through the medium of his Holiness, in whom we truly believe that he has revived for us the happy memory of Pope Alexander." Machiavelli, however, took a more realistic view of the situation: "Others . . . think that, inasmuch as the Pontiff had need of the Duke in his election, and having made him great promises therefore, he finds it advisable now to feed the Duke on hope. . . . And it is not to be supposed that Julius II will so quickly have forgotten the ten years of exile [in France] which he had to endure under Pope Alexander VI." In fact, Cesare's decision to support Julius was the only political maneuver for which Machiavelli was to

The fall of this formidable man, who had caused the whole of Italy to tremble, and whose name and fame had spread throughout the world, delivered Pope Julius II from a claimant who might one day have proved fatal to him.
—FERDINAND GREGOROVIUS
on Cesare Borgia

criticize him in *The Prince*. Indeed, Machiavelli's condemnation of Cesare in this regard was completely uncompromising. Cesare had, in Machiavelli's opinion, made the mistake of believing that "with great men new services wipe out old injuries." "The duke's choice," he wrote, "was a mistaken one; and it was the cause of his ultimate ruin."

The man whom Cesare had so unwisely chosen to trust was determined to restore the Church's authority throughout the Papal States. Julius did not, however, consider Cesare a suitable instrument of papal policy. He soon made it clear that he considered the restoration of the Borgias to supremacy in the Romagna just as undesirable as Venetian interference in the region.

The uncertainty of this situation began to take its toll on Cesare. Machiavelli found him much changed from the proud and self-assured person whose exploits at Senigallia had been the talk of all Italy just 10 months earlier.

The mighty Roman fortress of Castel Sant'Angelo, where Cesare and Alexander had taken refuge at a critical moment during the French invasion of Italy in 1494. In 1501 Alexander, to safeguard against further coercion by the French, had ordered improvements to the castle's fortifications.

On November 9, 1503, Julius met with his cardinals. To Cesare's dismay, he failed to address the question of who would be the next captain general. Cesare's spirits improved a little just a few days later, when Julius ordered the Florentine government to allow Cesare's forces to pass through its territory en route to the Romagna. He became dejected again, however, when Julius showed no concern at the Florentines' refusal to comply.

At this point, Cesare's confidence collapsed completely. His cavalry forces were already deep inside Florentine territory, he had lost most of his cities in the Romagna, and the Venetians were at the gates of Faenza. Faced with this dire situation, Cesare decided that there was nothing to be gained by remaining in Rome and set out for the Romagna.

A few days later, news reached Rome that Faenza had surrendered to the Venetians. Julius, fearing that Venice might be on the verge of annexing the Romagna, demanded that Cesare cede his remaining Romagnol strongholds to the Church. When Cesare refused, the enraged Julius ordered that he be arrested and brought back to Rome.

On December 1 Cesare, a prisoner in his former apartments in the Vatican, heard that da Corella and the Borgias' remaining cavalry forces had been captured near Florence. He immediately admitted defeat and gave the pope's agents the passwords to the Romagnol castles that were still loyal to him. At the same time, the vindictive Julius could not resist kicking Cesare when he was down; he began to encourage Cesare's enemies to institute legal proceedings against him. Finally, when Cesare's *castellans* (castle wardens) at Cesena refused to surrender to the papal envoys, Julius imprisoned him in the Torre Borgia.

It was in this tower, where Alfonso Bisceglie had been murdered by da Corella three years before, that Cesare began to recover the confidence that Machiavelli had thought lost and gone forever. With his fortunes at their lowest ebb and his life endangered as never before, Cesare seemed almost to take comfort from the fact that he knew exactly where he stood. Free of the uncertainties of the previous

Raphael's painting of a cardinal captures the self-assurance that characterized many Renaissance Italian princes of the Church.

weeks, he declared to one of Julius's officials, "The more I am in adversity, the more I fortify my spirit."

Shortly after Cesare's imprisonment in the Torre Borgia, the Spanish cardinals who had remained loyal to him petitioned Julius for his release, suggesting that Cesare's castellans in the Romagna might protest the pope's policy by surrendering their strongholds to the Venetians. Spanish opposition to Julius grew more vocal at the end of December, when word reached Rome that de Córdoba had led Ferdinand's armies to a resounding victory over the French in Naples. With Spain now dominant in southern Italy, Julius realized that mistreating a prominent Spaniard like Cesare might not be to his advantage.

ART RESOURCE

One of the many magnificent murals by Pinturicchio that adorn the Borgia apartments in the Vatican. Cesare was imprisoned there by Pope Julius II in December 1503 for refusing to cede his castles to the papacy. Though freed two months later, Cesare remained under papal guard to ensure that he would surrender his castles.

On January 18, 1504, the pope agreed to free Cesare on condition that he cede his Romagnol castles to the Church within 40 days. Despite this diplomatic victory, Julius felt uneasy. He complained that Cesare was "false, and that he could find no reality in him, and that in this matter he had made so many double plays that [he] did not know what foundation to put on it." On February 15, as a result of further intercessions by the Spanish cardinals, Cesare left the Torre Borgia for Ostia, where he was to remain in custody until the Romagnol fortresses had been surrendered to the Church. Following the capitulation of his castellans at Cesena and Bertinoro on April 15, Cesare was allowed to go free, and arrived in Naples on April 28, where he was greeted warmly by de Córdoba.

Freedom and fine weather greatly aided Cesare's recovery from the trials and tribulations of the previous months, and his partisans began to regain the confidence they had enjoyed prior to their master's period of misfortune. One of them commenced a recruiting drive for a campaign in the Romagna, declaring that his lord "would soon return to good standing and give his enemies food for thought."

98

Fortunately for Cesare's opponents, they were never put to this particular test. On the evening before he was to leave Naples, Cesare was arrested by de Córdoba, who was acting on the orders of Ferdinand and Isabella. The Spanish monarchs believed that having Cesare firmly within their camp would enable them to intimidate the pope into looking favorably upon their two most pressing problems — their claim to Naples and the papal dispensation that would permit their daughter Catherine of Aragon to marry Henry VIII of England, her deceased husband's brother.

Cesare had been reduced to the status of a pawn in the complex negotiations between the papacy and Spain. In despair, Cesare acceded to the pope's request that he relinquish his last possession in the Romagna, the fortress of Rocca di Forlì. With that act there remained nothing of the Borgia duchy that Cesare had hoped to make a model principality. On August 16, 1504, Cesare was escorted aboard a ship bound for Spain, where he was to be imprisoned, perhaps indefinitely, at Ferdinand and Isabella's pleasure.

Upon his arrival in Spain, Cesare was taken immediately to the mountain fortress of Chinchilla, deep in a remote region of the province of Valencia.

A 16th-century drawing of Naples, the city to which Cesare traveled following his release from papal custody in April 1504. There, on May 26, Cesare's hopes of winning Spanish support for his plans to regain the Romagna were dashed when the Spanish commander in Naples arrested him on the orders of Ferdinand and Isabella.

ICHNOGRAPHIA NEAPOLIS.

GOLFO   DI   NAPOLI.

There, he was informed that Ferdinand and Isabella planned to have him tried for the murders of Juan Borgia and Alfonso Bisceglie.

At the end of October 1504 Lucrezia Borgia, Cesare's brother-in-law Jean d'Albret, king of Navarre, and several Spanish churchmen complained to Ferdinand about his treatment of Cesare. The king responded by ordering improvements to Cesare's cell and allowing him more servants. Ferdinand also announced that Cesare would go free just as soon as he had been cleared of any involvement in the murders of Juan and Bisceglie.

By early 1505 the suspense and boredom of imprisonment had become more than Cesare could bear. He tried to escape by tying his bedsheets together to form a makeshift rope and then lowering himself from the window of his cell. The attempt failed dismally. The knotted sheets ripped and Cesare fell into the deep defensive ditch that surrounded the castle, fracturing his shoulder.

A few months later Cesare was transferred to the supposedly escape-proof Homenaje Tower at La

Ferdinand and Isabella accept the surrender of Muhammad XI, sultan of Granada, in 1492, thus ending the centuries-old Arab occupation of southern Spain.

Mota Castle, in the Castilian city of Medina del Campo. Confinement in this top-security prison was, in some ways, a tribute to his importance. This became even more apparent shortly after his transfer, when a fierce struggle for possession of the prisoner erupted between Ferdinand and Archduke Philip, son of the Holy Roman emperor, Maximilian I, and husband to Juana, one of Ferdinand and Isabella's daughters.

Philip and Ferdinand had been at odds since Isabella's death in November 1504. Because Juana's mental instability made her unfit to rule, Isabella had appointed Ferdinand regent of Castile on condition that he relinquish the regency should he remarry. Philip and Juana's son, Charles, would remain the undisputed heir to the Spanish throne (as a grandson of Ferdinand and Isabella), and to the Holy Roman Empire (through his father).

Ferdinand, whose dislike of the Habsburgs (the Holy Roman imperial family), had always stood in great contrast to Isabella's conviction that the imperial dynasts were useful allies, persuaded the Spanish legislative assembly to invalidate the remarriage clause in Isabella's will, and then struck a bargain with another European monarch who hated the Habsburgs — Louis XII of France. Louis promised Ferdinand the hand in marriage of his niece, Germaine de Foix, along with a very substantial dowry — the portion of Naples ceded to France under the terms of the Treaty of Granada. Louis also promised to help Ferdinand conquer Navarre on the condition that the kingdom pass to Gaston de Foix, Germaine's brother, upon Ferdinand's death.

Following his marriage to Germaine on March 18, 1506, Ferdinand ceded Castile to Philip and Juana and then secretly drew up a statement to the effect that he had done so under pressure and that he considered Philip to have usurped the regency from Juana. Ferdinand then prepared to depart for Naples, where de Córdoba, who was now his viceroy, was rumored to be negotiating with Emperor Maximilian in hopes of gaining Habsburg support for independent ventures in Italy. Ferdinand believed

AP WIDE WORLD PHOTOS

Cesare's sister, Lucrezia Borgia, pressured Ferdinand of Aragon to release Cesare from confinement. Although Lucrezia was embroiled in the intrigues of the Borgia family for most of her lifetime, she devoted the last years of her life to charitable pursuits and the cultivation of a brilliant court that supported Renaissance scholars and artists such as Cardinal Bembo and Titian.

Holy Roman Emperor Maximilian I, whose agents engineered Cesare's escape from imprisonment in Spain in 1506. Cesare believed that only in alliance with the immensely powerful Maximilian would he be able to recover his former possessions in Italy.

that Cesare might be a useful ally should he decide to mount an expedition against de Córdoba. Cesare's reappearance on the Italian scene would, thought Ferdinand, act as a catalyst. Political passions — the raw material with which statesmen work — would be aroused throughout the entire Italian peninsula.

Unfortunately for Ferdinand, Archduke Philip also recognized Cesare's potential usefulness. His refusal to hand Cesare over to Ferdinand undoubtedly had much to do with the fact that Cesare had secretly been in communication with Philip's partisans in Medina del Campo for some time and had decided to ally himself with the Habsburgs. Cesare recognized that the Habsburgs were the one European power strong enough to intimidate Julius, to dictate to the princes of Italy, and to overwhelm the Franco-Spanish coalition. Cesare now believed that only in alliance with the Holy Roman Empire would he stand a chance of recovering his former possessions. He sent word to his brother-in-law, Jean d'Albret, king of Navarre, that an alliance with the Habsburgs might be in his best interests too. The situation became critical when Archduke Philip died of influenza on September 25, 1506. The Habsburg lobby at the Castilian court decided that Cesare should go to the Netherlands via Navarre and return with Philip and Juana's son, Charles, the rightful heir to the crown of Castile.

Although the interests of Navarre, Cesare, and the Holy Roman Empire were, to some extent, in harmony, there was still a major obstacle to the active pursuit of this proposed policy — Cesare's imprisonment. Accordingly, the Habsburgs' agents set about bribing the chaplain whose services Cesare had been allowed by the governor of the castle.

On the night of October 25, 1506, Cesare found himself once again descending a rope in darkness. This time, however, it was not the weakness of the rope that almost caused his death. The jailers at La Mota, who were among the most security conscious in Spain, had discovered Cesare's absence during a routine check. Storming into the room, they ran to the window and cut the rope. Cesare hit the ground with a thud that convinced the horsemen waiting to spirit him away that he must have been killed. However, when the motionless figure sprawled before them began to emit a string of curses, his rescuers bundled him onto a horse and sped away into the night.

On December 3, 1506, after a grueling ride through harsh and mountainous country, Cesare arrived in Pamplona, the capital of Navarre, where he was greeted by d'Albret, who had no doubt that Cesare would prove to be an immense asset both as a commander in the Navarrese armies and as a politician of international repute whose influence abroad would aid the Navarrese in their search for profitable alliances.

Cesare soon began to exercise his political imagination on the kind of scale that had made him the living legend he was. Convinced that a good record of service in pro-Habsburg Navarre could lead to a senior command with Maximilian's armies, he gave much thought to the advantages that he might stand to gain in light of the emperor's recent announcement that he intended to descend upon Rome and force Julius II to crown him officially.

Convinced that he was soon to regain the international limelight, Cesare began to make plans for the expedition to the Netherlands. At the same time, he and d'Albret set about improving Navarre's defenses, since they suspected that a combined Franco-Spanish invasion was imminent. The Netherlands project was shelved, however, at the end of December, when civil war broke out. Luis de Beaumonte y Luza, constable of Navarre and a supporter of Ferdinand, refused to declare obedience to d'Albret, thus continuing his policy of flouting d'Albret's authority and using his fortress at Viana as a base for operations against the Navarrese nobility. D'Albret had tolerated the constable's pro-Spanish stance for almost two years, but now, with Viana vital to the defense of Navarre, he considered de Beaumonte y Luza's policy tantamount to treason.

In February 1507 Cesare rode out of Pamplona at the head of an army of 6,000 men. In the wake of an abortive siege at Larriaga, where resistance had

So it should be noted that when he seizes a state the new ruler must determine all the injuries that he will need to inflict. He must inflict them once for all, and not have to renew them every day, and in that way he will be able to set men's minds at rest and win them over to him when he confers benefits.
—NICCOLÒ MACHIAVELLI

Cesare's last battle had none of the grandeur or magnitude of the engagement portrayed by Paolo Uccello in his *The Battle of San Egidio*. The 32-year-old Cesare was killed on March 12, 1507, near Viana, Navarre, in a skirmish with three knights.

been much tougher than anticipated, Cesare decided that the Navarrese war effort should be concentrated against the very focus of the rebellion — Viana, where d'Albret was already encamped and attempting to starve the garrison into submission.

Situated on high ground a short distance to the east of the town, the fortress of Viana was manned by troops under the command of de Beaumonte y Luza's son. The constable himself had decided to make his stand at Mendavia, a few miles to the southeast. Between the two bastions stretched some of the dreariest terrain in all Navarre — a succession of bare sandstone hills broken only by deep and twisting gullies known as *barrancos*.

When Cesare arrived at Viana, early in March 1507, he was still not accustomed to the Navarrese way of waging war. As a veteran of several campaigns in civilized and sophisticated Italy, he had not yet completely discarded his tendency to regard the Navarrese military as somewhat primitive and decidedly provincial. His concern with the comfort of his troops, which was understandable in a former commander of mercenary forces, both amused and disturbed the Navarrese, who were a tough and hardy people, seemingly impervious to the privations of life in the field.

On the night of March 11, 1507, Cesare's previous experience proved to be his undoing. Confronted with a ferocious rainstorm, he permitted his troops to shelter in the town, reckoning it impossible that de Beaumonte y Luza would attempt to send a supply train from Mendavia to Viana in such abysmal weather.

The wily constable had been waiting for just such an opportunity. Under cover of darkness and storm, a supply train from Mendavia reached Viana. A few hours later, just as dawn broke, the 60 horsemen who had accompanied the supply train set out on their return journey. They had only ridden a few hundred yards when they spotted a cavalry detachment charging toward them. These were reinforcements that had recently been promised to them by one of de Beaumonte y Luza's allies. The constable's men began to cheer, and cries of "*Beaumonte! Beaumonte!*" echoed across the barrancos.

Hearing this commotion, Cesare's troops immediately sounded the alarm. Their leader, furious at having been outmaneuvered, quickly donned light armor, grabbed his lance, and strode out into the courtyard of his residence, where his grooms were feverishly saddling his warhorse.

On this occasion, Cesare was unable to contain and concentrate his passions. He resented the fact that the Viana campaign had delayed his departure for the Netherlands, and he suspected that d'Albret's original approval of his decision to allow his troops to shelter in the town would turn to criticism in the wake of the tactical victory that de Beaumonte y Luza had gained from it.

In a rage, Cesare thundered down the road to Mendavia, roaring out his challenge to d'Albret's enemies. Great spots of his horse's blood spattered the ground and discolored the puddles as he raked the creature's flanks with his spurs. De Beaumonte y Luza, who had ridden up to meet with the returning escorts, ordered three of his knights to waylay the lone rider. Cesare ran straight into the

> *Whenever men are not obliged by necessity to fight, they fight from ambition.*
> —NICCOLÒ MACHIAVELLI

Three drawings of Cesare Borgia by Leonardo da Vinci. When news of Cesare's death reached Italy, his immediate family mourned, while his enemies were jubilant. Reactions of a different kind were forthcoming from Italy's poets, one of whom, Geronimo Casio, wrote: "Cesare Borgia, whom all / For force of arms and valor / regarded as a sun. . . ."

ambush and was unhorsed by a terrible lance thrust. Although mortally injured, he fought like a madman. Finally, with stab wounds all over his body, the former scourge of civilized Italy fell to the ground. His life's blood drained away into the sandy soil of a poor and primitive kingdom hundreds of miles from the city and civilization where he had known his greatest fame and fortune. He was 32 years old.

Jean d'Albret, distraught at the death of his brother-in-law, had Cesare's body brought back to Viana and buried in the Church of Santa Maria. The inscription carved upon the marble tomb which the Navarrese later erected over Cesare's grave read: "Here lies he whom all the world feared."

Among the very few people who grieved for Cesare, perhaps none were more sincere than his wife, his sister, and his mother. Charlotte, his wife, who had never seen Cesare again after his departure from France, went into mourning for the rest of her life and led an existence of somber serenity despite the fact that she was beautiful, wealthy, and just 25 years old when Cesare was killed. Lucrezia resigned herself to a life in which her brother would no longer play a part, and made the most of her position as duchess of Ferrara. Vannozza, having survived her tragic association with the Borgias, went on to become a woman of property. When she died in 1518, she received a funeral as grand as any cardinal's.

History's judgment of Cesare Borgia remains ambiguous at best, and probably always will be. If the great men of the Renaissance can best be assessed by the standards of their time, then this Renaissance prince at the mention of whose name the mighty trembled must be accounted a man of considerable stature.

Cesare often understood his enemies better than they understood themselves. He saw men as they were, not as they wished to be considered. He took careful note of his opponents' strengths and then went straight for the jugular of their weaknesses. Rarely allowing considerations of humanity to color his political judgment, he believed that political gains are best secured by the willingness to resort to cruelty and deceit should no other method seem likely to suffice. Cesare was, in fact, living proof of the validity of Machiavelli's assertion that "it is far better to be feared than loved if you cannot be both." He epitomized the spirit of a period during which the ruling classes believed that a man could do anything as long as he possessed sufficient willpower.

To judge Cesare by what he did achieve rather than by what he hoped to achieve is to miss the point. His appreciation of the political capital that might have been made from the unification of the Papal States and the creation of a model duchy in the Romagna was, in terms of place and period, truly revolutionary.

In the final analysis, it is because he was the model for Machiavelli's ideal prince that Cesare remains the subject of study to this day. Just as they have for more than 450 years, scholars and statesmen alike in centuries to come will find themselves pondering the implications of Machiavelli's assertion that "[if] all the achievements of [Cesare Borgia] are considered, it will be found that he built up a great substructure for his future power; nor do I know what precepts I could furnish to a prince in his commencement better than those that are to be derived from his example."

So having summed up all that he did, I cannot possibly censure him. Rather, I think I have been right in putting him forward as an example for all those who have acquired power through good fortune and the arms of others. He was a man of great courage and high intentions.
—NICCOLÒ MACHIAVELLI
on Cesare Borgia

Further Reading

Bradford, S. *Cesare Borgia: His Life and Times.* London: Weidenfeld and Nicolson, 1976.

Burckhardt, Jacob. *The Civilization of the Renaissance in Italy,* trans. S. G. C. Middlemore. New York: Harper and Row Publishers, Inc., 1929.

Castiglione, Baldesar. *The Book of the Courtier,* trans. George Bull. Harmondsworth, Middlesex: Penguin Books, Ltd., 1967.

Hauser, Ernest O. *Italy: A Cultural Guide.* New York: Atheneum, 1981.

Hearder, H. and D. P. Waley, eds. *A Short History of Italy from Classical Times to the Present Day.* Cambridge: Cambridge University Press, 1963.

Machiavelli, Niccolò. *The Discourses,* trans. Leslie J. Walker, S.J., ed. Bernard Crick. Harmondsworth, Middlesex: Penguin Books, Ltd., 1970.

————. *The Prince,* trans. George Bull. Harmondsworth, Middlesex: Penguin Books, Ltd., 1961.

Mallett, M. *The Borgias: The Rise and Fall of a Renaissance Dynasty.* London: The Bodley Head, Ltd., 1969.

Martines, Lauro. *Power and Imagination: City-States in Renaissance Italy.* New York: Alfred A. Knopf, Inc., 1979.

Prescott, Orville. *Princes of the Renaissance.* New York: Random House, Inc., 1969.

Southern, R. W. *Western Society and the Church in the Middle Ages.* Harmondsworth, Middlesex: Penguin Books, Ltd., 1970.

Chronology

Sept. 1475	Born Cesare Borgia, to Vannozza de'Cattanei, mistress of Cardinal Rodrigo Borgia, in Rome
1489	Studies law at University of Perugia Appointed bishop-elect of Pamplona
Sept. 1491	Commences doctoral studies at University of Pisa
1492	Rodrigo Borgia elected pope and takes office as Alexander VI; appoints Cesare archbishop of Valencia
Sept. 20, 1493	Alexander VI appoints Cesare cardinal of Valencia
Sept. 3, 1494	Charles VIII of France invades Italy
June 1497	Murder of Cesare's brother, Juan, possibly on Cesare's orders
Aug. 1498	Sacred College approves Cesare's renunciation of cardinalate Cesare created duke of Valence and Diois by Louis XII of France
1499	Marries Charlotte d'Albret, sister of Jean d'Albret, king of Navarre Campaigns in Italy as senior commander with armies of France
March 29, 1500	Appointed captain general of the Church
Aug. 18, 1500	Alfonso Bisceglie, Cesare's brother-in-law, murdered on Cesare's orders
Oct. 1, 1500	Cesare commences first Romagna campaign
May 15, 1501	Invested with title of duke of Romagna by Alexander VI
June 1502	Commences second Romagna campaign
Aug. 18, 1503	Cesare's father, Pope Alexander VI, dies of malaria
Oct. 8, 1503	Cesare reappointed captain general of the Church by Pope Pius III
Oct. 17, 1503	Death of Pius III
Dec. 1503–Apr. 1504	Cesare imprisoned by Pope Julius II
Sept. 1504	Arrives in Spain as prisoner of Ferdinand of Aragon and Isabella of Castile
1505	Transferred to fortress of La Mota
Oct. 25, 1506	Escapes from La Mota
Dec. 3, 1506	Arrives in Navarre to join forces with the king, his brother-in-law, Jean d'Albret
March 12, 1507	Killed in action at Viana, fighting Navarrese supporters of Ferdinand of Aragon

Index

John Haney graduated from London University in 1976 with an honors degree in Classics. Between 1977 and 1981 he worked as a recording and performing artist with a contemporary music ensemble, regularly touring the United States and Europe. A resident of New York since 1982, he now works as an editor, writer, and lyricist. He spends most of his spare time studying the history of Soviet Russia.

Arthur M. Schlesinger, jr., taught history at Harvard for many years and is currently Albert Schweitzer Professor of the Humanities at City University of New York. He is the author of numerous highly praised works in American history and has twice been awarded the Pulitzer Prize. He served in the White House as special assistant to Presidents Kennedy and Johnson.